Gleanings from the Past

Volume 3

Extracts from the Writings of Thomas Watson

Selected by Hamilton Smith

Scripture Truth Publications

EXTRACTS FROM THE WRITINGS OF THOMAS WATSON

Paperback and hardback editions first published 1915 by The Central Bible Truth Depôt, 12 Paternoster Row, London, E.C.
Re-typeset and transferred to Digital Printing 2009
ISBN: 978-0-901860-83-5 (paperback)
Copyright © 1915 The Central Bible Truth Depôt and 2009 Scripture Truth Publications in this edition

A publication of Scripture Truth

All rights reserved. No part of this publication may be reproduced, stored in a retrieval system, or transmitted, in any form or by any means, electronic, mechanical, photocopying, recording or otherwise without prior permission of Scripture Truth Publications.

Scripture quotations are taken from The Authorized (King James) Version. Rights in the Authorized Version are vested in the Crown. Reproduced by permission of the Crown's patentee, Cambridge University Press.

Cover photograph ©iStockphoto.com/iacon (Jeffery Borchert)

Published by Scripture Truth Publications
31-33 Glover Street, Crewe, Cheshire, CW1 3LD

Scripture Truth is an imprint of Central Bible Hammond Trust, a charitable trust

Digital copy provided by Les Hodgett
Typesetting by John Rice
Printed and bound by Lightning Source

EXTRACTS FROM THE WRITINGS OF THOMAS WATSON

Preface

The servant of the Lord, from whose writings these extracts have been culled, prefaced one of his works by saying, "There are two things which I have always looked upon as difficult: the one is to make the wicked sad; the other is to make the godly joyful." Alas! This sad world still holds many a careless sinner, and not a few sorrowful saints, though two hundred and fifty years have passed since these words were uttered. May God so speed this little book, that, in His good hand, it may be the means of arousing some sleeping conscience, and dropping a word of cheer into some sorrowful heart.

Hamilton Smith
1915

EXTRACTS FROM THE WRITINGS OF THOMAS WATSON

EXTRACTS FROM THE WRITINGS OF THOMAS WATSON

Contents

	Page
Preface	3
Biographical Introduction	7

Chapter

1. Warnings 11
2. Healing 20
3. Giving 24
4. Longing 27
5. Contentment 31
6. Poverty 36
7. Afflictions 41
8. Persecution 48
9. Temptation 56
10. Contention 61
11. Preaching 64
12. Praying 68
13. Meditation 71
14. Departing 78
15. Crowning 83
16. Fragments 87

EXTRACTS FROM THE WRITINGS OF THOMAS WATSON

Biographical Introduction

Comparatively little is known of the personal history of Thomas Watson. We know nothing of his parentage, and are quite ignorant of the time and place of his birth, or where his early years were spent.

His name appears in Kennet's "Register and Chronicle", as one of a number of other famous Puritan ministers educated at Emmanuel College, Cambridge, and, tradition reports, that, while at Cambridge, he was a most laborious student.

It would appear that after leaving the University, he lived for some time with the family of Mary, the widow of Sir Horace Vere, baron of Tilbury.

In 1646 Watson married Abigail daughter of John Beadle, the rector of Barnston, Essex. In the same year he was appointed rector of the parish of St. Stephen's, Walbrook. He became highly esteemed in the City of London as a man of considerable learning, a popular preacher, and a man of personal piety and prayer. Calamy, in his "Abridgements", relates that on a certain day when Watson was in the pulpit, "among other hearers, there came in that Reverend and learned Prelate, Bishop Richardson, who was so well pleased with his sermon, but especially with his prayer after it, that he followed him home, to give him thanks; and earnestly desired a copy of his prayer. 'Alas!' said Mr. Watson, 'that is what I cannot give; for I do not use to pen my prayers; it was no studied thing, but uttered as God enabled me from the abundance of my heart and affections, *pro re nata* [1].' Upon which the good Bishop went away wondering that any man could pray in that manner, *ex tempore* [2]." From this little incident we may judge that Thomas Watson realised the truth of Rutherford's touching words, "There be so many other things that are a-pouring out of the soul in prayer; as groaning, sighing, looking up to heaven, breathing, weeping; that it cannot be imagined, how far short printed and read prayers come of vehement praying: for you cannot put sighs, groans, tears, breathing, and such heart-messengers down in a printed book; nor can paper and ink lay your heart, in all its sweet affections, out before God."

During the Civil War, Watson inclined strongly to Presbyterian views. He joined some sixty Presbyterian ministers in an appeal to Cromwell, declaring their abhorrence of all violence against the person of the King, and urging him, and his army, to have no concern in it.

In 1651 he allowed himself to become involved, with others, in political correspondence with Charles II, then in Holland, and spent some months in the Tower for his pains.

On regaining his liberty he continued his charge at St. Stephen's until the passing of the Act of Uniformity in 1662. By this intolerant Act upwards of two thousand clergy were driven from their parishes; among them the

[1] as the situation demands
[2] without following a script

BIOGRAPHICAL INTRODUCTION

wisest and most godly in the land. For conscience' sake the greater part of these ejected ministers had, henceforth, to face poverty and reproach, suffering and trial.

Thomas Watson was one of the London ejected ministers. His touching farewell address is still extant. The closing paragraph is worth quoting:

"The hour is come wherein the sun is setting on not a few of the prophets: our work seems to be at an end; our pulpits and places must know us no more. You are not ignorant what things there are imposed on us as the condition of our continuing our ministration. I must profess before God, angels, and men, that my non-submission is not from any disloyalty to authority or any factious disposition, but because I dare not do anything concerning which my heart tells me the Lord says, 'Do it not.' I feel I must part with my conscience or with my ministry. I choose, therefore, that my ministry be sealed up by my sufferings, rather than be lengthened out by a lie; but I shall, through the grace of God, endeavour patiently and peaceably to suffer as a Christian. And now welcome the cross of Christ; welcome reproach; welcome poverty, scorn, and contempt, or whatever may befall me. This morning I had a flock and you had a pastor, but now behold a pastor without a flock, and a flock without a shepherd! This morning, I had a house, now I have none. This morning, I had a living, now I have none: 'The Lord gave, and the Lord hath taken away, blessed be the name of the Lord.' And thus, brethren, I bid you all farewell. 'Finally, brethren, farewell.'"

After his ejectment he continued to exercise his ministry in a private way. Following upon the Fire of London in 1666, he fitted up a large room for preaching, and later, at the time of the Declaration of Indulgence in 1672, he obtained a license for the use of the great hall of Crosby House, then belonging to Sir John Langham, a patron of evangelical nonconformity.

After preaching there for several years, his health gave way and he left the City for the quiet of Barnston in Essex. His end came suddenly in 1686, while engaged in prayer in his private room. He was buried on 28th July, 1686, in the grave of his father-in-law, John Beadle.

Hamilton Smith

1.
Warnings

"Seek ye the LORD while He may be found, call ye upon Him while He is near."—ISAIAH 55:6

Sin is the source of our sorrows, and the grave of our comforts. Sin is the sinner's bond (Acts 8:23), and the saint's burden (Psalm 38:3).

Little sins (suppose them so) yet multiplied become great. What is less than a grain of sand? yet when multiplied, what is heavier than the sand of the sea? A little sum multiplied is great; a little sin, unrepented of, will damn; as one leak in the ship, if it be not looked to, will sink it. You would think it is no great matter to forget God, yet it hath a heavy doom (Psalm 50:22).

It is sad to have old age and old sins. It is hard to pull up an old tree that is rooted, it is easier to cut it down for the fire.

PROCRASTINATION

When the lamp is almost out, the strength exhausted, and old age comes on, then mourning for sin will be in season. Men do not argue thus in other cases; they do not say, it is too soon to be rich; they will not put off the getting of riches to old age; no, here they take the first opportunity. When God calls for mourning and thou art deaf, when thou callest for mercy God may be dumb (Proverbs 1:24, 28). God may take the latter time to judge thee in because thou didst not take the former time to repent in. Though true mourning for sin be never too late, yet late mourning is seldom true. That repentance is seldom true-hearted which is grey-headed. The mariner in a storm throws his goods overboard, not but that he loves them, but he is afraid they will sink the ship; when men fall to weeping, work late, and would cast their sins overboard, it is for the most part only for fear lest they should sink the ship and drown in hell.

Old age is no good age to repent in. A tender plant is easily removed, but it is hard to pluck up an old tree that is rooted. It were a very unwise course for a mariner, while the ship is sound, the tackling strong, the wind favourable, the sea calm, to lie idle at anchor; and when the ship begins to leak, and the tempest to rise, now to launch forth and hoist up sails for a voyage; so is he who neglects the time of health and strength, and when old age comes, and his tackling is even broken, now begins his voyage towards heaven. How unworthy is this, for men to give the devil their strength and marrow, and then come and lay their old bones upon God's altar? A sinner in the time of his old age, sleeps between death and the devil. It is just, that he who forgets God in the time of health, God should forget him in the time of sickness.

False peace

"When a strong man armed keepeth his palace, his goods are in peace" (Luke 11:21). This is the devil's peace; he rocks men in the cradle of security; he cries Peace, peace, when men are on the precipice of hell. The seeming peace a sinner has, is not from the knowledge of his happiness, but from the ignorance of his danger. ... True peace is after trouble. God convinces and humbles the soul; then He speaks peace. Many say they have peace, but is this peace before a storm, or after it? True peace is after trouble. First there was the earthquake, and then the fire, and then the still small voice (1 Kings 19:12). God pours the golden oil of peace into broken hearts.

FALSE REPENTANCE

Many think they repent when it is not the offence, but the penalty troubles them; not the treason but the blood-axe. Some think they repent when they shed a few tears, as Saul did for his unkindness to David, "And Saul lifted up his voice and wept. And he said to David ... thou hast rewarded me good, whereas I have rewarded thee evil" (1 Samuel 24:16-17). But for all this he follows David again. So men can lift up their voice and weep for sins, yet follow their sins again. Others forsake their sin, but still retain their love for it in their hearts, like the snake that casts the coat but keeps the sting.

"Blessed are they that mourn: for they shall be comforted" (Matthew 5:4). We must go through the valley of tears to Paradise. Mourning were a sad subject to treat on, were it not that it hath blessedness going before, and comfort coming after.

There is a mourning that is far from making one blessed. Many can weep over a dead child that cannot mourn over a crucified Saviour. Worldly sorrows hasten our funerals. "The sorrow of the world worketh death" (2 Corinthians 7:10).

There is a despairing kind of mourning; such was Judas' mourning: he saw his sin, he was sorry, he justified Christ, he made restitution. Judas, who is in hell, did more than many nowadays; well, wherein was Judas' sorrow blameworthy? It was a mourning joined with despair; he thought his wound broader than the plaster; his was not "repentance unto life" (Acts 11:18), but rather unto death.

There is a hypocritical mourning: the heart is very deceitful, it can betray as well as by a tear as by a kiss: Saul looks like a mourner, and as he was sometimes among the prophets (1 Samuel 10:12), so he seemed to be among the penitents, "And Saul said unto Samuel, I have sinned, for I have transgressed the commandment of the LORD" (1 Samuel 15:24). Saul did play the hypocrite in his mourning; for he did not take shame to himself, but he did rather take honour to himself. "Honour me before the elders of the people." How easy it is for a man to put a cheat upon his soul, and by hypocrisy to weep himself into hell.

There is a forced mourning when tears are pumped out by God's judgments. Such was Cain's mourning: "My punishment is greater than I can bear" (Genesis 4:13). His punishment troubled him more than his sin; to mourn only for the fear of hell, is like a thief who weeps for the penalty, rather than the offence. A sinner mourns because judgment follows at the heel of sin; but David cries out, "My sin is ever before me" (Psalm 51:3). The prodigal saith, "I have sinned against heaven, and before thee." He doth not say, "I am almost starved among the husks", but "I have offended my Father."

It is an excellent saying of St. Austin [1], "He doth truly bewail the sins he hath committed, who never commits the sins he hath bewailed."

A child of God will confess sin in particular; an unsound Christian will confess sin by wholesale, he will acknowl-

---

[1] Also known as Augustine of Hippo or St. Augustine

edge that he is a sinner in general; whereas David doth, as it were, point with his finger to the sore (Psalm 51:4): "I have done this evil"; he doth not say, I have done evil, but this evil.

To die is to be but once done, and after death there is nothing to be done. If thou diest in thine impenitency there is no repenting in the grave. If thou leavest thy work at death half done, there is no finishing it in the grave (Ecclesiastes 9:10): "There is no work, nor device, nor wisdom in the grave whither thou goest."

God hath given thee two eyes, if thou losest one, thou hast another; but thou hast but one soul, and if thou art robbed of that, thou art undone for ever.

The grave buries all a sinner's joy. They have a short feast, but a long reckoning. The time being short, the sinning time cannot be long.

Sinners, the time is shortly coming when the drawbridge of mercy will be quite pulled up. "Because sentence against an evil work is not executed speedily, therefore the heart of the sons of men is fully set in them to do evil" (Ecclesiastes 8:11). God forbears punishing, therefore men forbear repenting. God is not only gracious, but He waits to be gracious (Isaiah 30:18). But though men will not set bounds to their sin, yet God sets bounds to His patience. God saith, "My Spirit shall not always strive with man." The angel cried, "the hour of His judgment is come" (Revelation 14:7).

If Felix trembled when Paul preached of judgment (Acts 24:25), how will sinners tremble when they shall see Christ come to judgment!

If God lets men prosper awhile in their sin, His vial of wrath is all this while filling; His sword is all this time whetting: and though God may forbear men a while, yet long forbearance is no forgiveness. The longer God is in taking His blow, the heavier it will be at last. As long as there is eternity, God has time enough to reckon with His enemies.

Knowledge without affection

Men have notions of Christ, but are not warmed with love to Christ. Their knowledge is like the moon, it hath light in it, but no heat. The knowledge that hypocrites have of Christ, hath no saving influence upon them, it doth not make them more holy: it is one thing to have a notion of Christ, another thing to fetch virtue from Christ. The knowledge of hypocrites is a dead, barren knowledge: it is informing, but not transforming; it doth not make them a jot the better. ... "Thy wisdom and thy knowledge, it hath perverted thee" (Isaiah 47:10); the knowledge of most makes them more cunning in sin; these have little cause to glory in their knowledge. Absalom might boast of the hair of his head, but that hanged him; so these may boast of the knowledge of their head, but it will destroy them. Many of the old world knew there was an ark, but were drowned, because they did not get into the ark; knowledge which is not applying, will but light a man to hell.

The show of holiness

All our pompous show of holiness without sincerity, is but folly set forth in its embroidery; it is but going to hell in a more devout way than others. ... The upright man hath no subterfuges, his tongue and his heart go together, he is downright upright. ... Men are ambitious of credit, and would gain repute in the world, therefore they will dress themselves in the garb and mode of religion, that others may write them down for saints. But alas, what is one the better to have others to commend him, and his conscience condemn him? What good will it do a man when he is in hell, that others think he is gone to heaven? Counterfeit piety is double iniquity. The hypocrite deceives others while he lives, but deceives himself when he dies. The hypocrite is abhorred of all. Wicked men hate him because he makes a show, and God hates him because he doth but make a show: the wicked hate him because he hath so much a show of godliness, and God hates him because he hath no more (Acts 26:28).

EMPTY PROFESSION

What is a man the better to have Christ's name upon him, if he still retain Satan's image? What is he advantaged to have the oracles of God, and want the Spirit of God? Think not that an empty profession will save; millions will be sent to hell in Christ's livery (Matthew 7:22; 8:12).

THE CLOAK OF RELIGION

Sometimes covetousness pretends conscience; Judas fisheth for money under a pretence of religion: "Why was not this ointment sold for three hundred pence, and given to the poor?" (John 12:5). How charitable Judas was! but his charity began at home, for he carried the bag. Many make religion a cloak for their ambition. "Come … see my zeal", saith Jehu, "for the LORD" (2 Kings 10:16). No, Jehu, thy zeal was for the kingdom. It was not zeal, but state-policy. Jehu made religion hold the stirrup till he got possession of the crown.

Counterfeit piety is double iniquity. A little rusty gold is far better than a great deal of bright brass. A little true grace, though rusted over with many infirmities, is better than all the glistering shows of hypocrites. … The hypocrite is fair to look on, he hath a devout eye but a hollow heart; but he who is sincere, his inside is his best side.

Hypocrites will obey God in some things which are consistent either with their credit or profit, but in other things they desire to be excused: like Esau who obeyed his father in bringing him venison, because probably he liked the sport of hunting, but refused to obey him in a business of greater importance, namely, in the choice of his wife.

Hypocrites will not sail in a storm; true grace holds out in the winter season. That is a precious faith, which, like the star, shines brightest in the darkest night.

No escape in judgment

If once the sentence of judgment is passed, what wilt thou do? Whither wilt thou go? Wilt thou seek help from God? He is "a consuming fire". Wilt thou seek help from the world? It will be all on fire about thee. From the saints? These thou didst deride upon earth! From thy conscience? There is the worm that gnaws. From Mercy? The lease is run out.

Whatever God can require for satisfaction, or we can need for salvation, is to be found in Christ. His name is the sweetest music to a Christian's ear, and His blood the most precious balm to a Christian's heart.

It is not money in a rich man's hand, though offered to us, that will enrich us, unless we receive it. So Christ's virtues or benefits will do us no good unless we receive them by the hand of faith.

Faith lives in a broken heart. "He cried out, and said with tears, Lord, I believe" (Mark 9:24). True faith is always in a heart bruised for sin.

Justifying faith lies in recumbency; we rest on Christ alone for salvation. As a man that is ready to drown catches hold on the bough of a tree, so a poor trembling sinner, seeing himself ready to perish, catches hold by faith on Christ, the tree of life, and is saved.

Of all sins, beware of the rock of unbelief. "Take heed lest there be in any of you an evil heart of unbelief" (Hebrews 3:12). Men think, as long as they are not drunkards or swearers, it is no great matter to be unbelievers. This is the gospel sin. It disparages Christ's infinite merit as if it would not save; it makes the wound of sin to be broader than the plaster of Christ's blood. This is high contempt offered to Christ, and is a deeper spear than that which the Jews thrust into His side.

God has depth of mercy, it reaches as low as sinners; and height of mercy, it reaches above the clouds. ... Take heed of abusing the mercy of God. Suck not poison out of the sweet flower of God's mercy. Think not that because God is merciful, you may go on in sin; this is to make mercy your enemy. To sin because mercy abounds is the devil's logic. He that sins because of mercy, is like one that wounds his head because he has a plaster. He that sins because of God's mercy, shall have judgment without mercy. Mercy abused turns to fury. If "he bless himself in his heart, saying, I shall have peace though I walk in the imagination of mine heart, to add drunkenness to thirst; the LORD will not spare him, but then the anger of the LORD, and His jealousy, shall smoke against that man" (Deuteronomy 29:19-20).

God has treasures of mercy; prayer is the key that opens these treasures; and in prayer be sure to carry Christ in your arms, for all the mercy comes through Christ. "Samuel took a sucking lamb" (1 Samuel 7:9).

2.
Healing

"He healeth the broken in heart, and bindeth up their wounds."—Psalm 147:3

Christ is the most skilful physician, there is no disease too hard for Him. "Who healeth all thy diseases" (Psalm 103:3).

Christ shows more love to His patients than any physician besides: which appears in that long journey He took from heaven to earth, and in that He comes to His patients without sending for, "I am sought of them that asked not for Me; I am found of them that sought Me not" (Isaiah 65:1). Then this physician lets Himself bleed to cure His patient, "He was wounded for our transgressions … and with His stripes we are healed" (Isaiah 53:5). Through His wounds we may see His bowels. Christ Himself drank that bitter cup which we should have drunk, and by His taking the potion we are healed and saved.

Christ is the most cheap physician, He takes no fee. "A woman having an issue of blood twelve years, which had spent *all her living* upon physicians … came behind Him and touched the border of His garment: and immediately her issue of blood stanched" (Luke 8:43-44). He desires us to bring nothing to Him but broken hearts; and when He hath cured us He desires us to bestow nothing upon Him but our love.

Christ heals with more ease than any other. Christ makes the devil go out with a word (Mark 9:25). Nay, He can cure with a look: Christ's look melted Peter into repentance; it was an healing look. If Christ doth but cast a look upon the soul He can recover it. Therefore David prays to have a look from God, "Look Thou upon me, and be merciful unto me" (Psalm 119:132).

Christ is the most tender-hearted physician. He hath ended His passion but not His compassion. He is not more full of skill than sympathy, "He healeth the broken in heart, and bindeth up their wounds" (Psalm 147:3). Every groan of the patient goes to the heart of this physician.

Christ never fails of success. Christ never undertakes to heal any but He makes a certain cure, "Those that Thou gavest Me I have kept, and none of them is lost" (John 17:12). Other physicians can only cure them that are sick, but Christ cures them that are dead, "And you hath He quickened who were dead in trespasses and sins" (Ephesians 2:1). Christ is a physician for the dead; of every one whom Christ cures, it may be said, "He was dead, and is alive again" (Luke 15:32).

Christ is the most bountiful physician. Other patients do enrich their physicians, but here the physician doth enrich the patient. Christ prefers all His patients: He doth not only cure them but crown them (Revelation 2:10). Christ doth not only raise from the bed, but to the throne; He gives the sick man not only health but heaven.

If Christ be a physician, then let us make use of this physician for our diseased souls. "When the sun was setting, all they that had any sick with divers diseases brought them unto Him, and He laid His hands on every one of them and healed them" (Luke 4:40). You that have neglected a physician all this while, now when the sun of the gospel, and the sun of your life, is even now setting, bring your sick souls to Christ to be cured. Christ complains that though men are sick unto death, yet they will not come or send to the physician, "Ye will not come to Me, that ye might have life" (John 5:40). But, object poor souls, "I am discouraged to go to Christ to ease me because of my unworthiness." Who did Christ shed His blood for but such as are unworthy? "Christ Jesus came into the world to save sinners" (1 Timothy 1:15). Christ came into the world as into an hospital among a company of lame, bed-rid souls. Who was ever yet saved because he was worthy? What man could ever plead this title, 'Lord Jesus, heal me, because I am worthy'? What worthiness was in Paul before his conversion? What worthiness in Mary Magdalen, out of whom seven devils were cast? But free-grace did pity and heal them; God does not find us worthy, but makes us worthy. If we never come to Christ to be healed till we are worthy, we must never come; and this talking of worthiness savours of pride, we would have something of our own; had we such preparations and self-excellencies then we think Christ would accept us, and we might come and be healed; this is to fee our physician; oh, let not the sense of unworthiness discourage; go to Christ to be healed. "Arise, He calleth thee" (Mark 10:49). Consider what a little time we have to stay here, and let that hasten the cure. Solomon saith there is "a time to be born, and a time to die" (Ecclesiastes 3:2), but mentions no time of living, as if that were so short it were not worth the naming. Oh, hasten the soul's cure, death is upon its swift march, and

HEALING

if that surprise you suddenly, there is no cure to be wrought in the grave. "Whatsoever thy hand findeth to do, do it with thy might; for there is no work, nor device, nor knowledge, nor wisdom, in the grave, whither thou goest" (Ecclesiastes 9:10). Now is the time of healing, now is the day of grace, now Christ pours out His balsam, "Now is the accepted time" (2 Corinthians 6:2). If we neglect the day of grace, the next will be a day of wrath (Romans 2:5).

If men will not receive the tenders of grace, Christ grieves (Mark 3:5). He is like a judge that passeth the sentence with tears in his eyes, "He beheld the city, and wept over it" (Luke 19:41). Ah, sinners, I come to save you, but you put away salvation from you: I come with healing under My wings, but you bolt out your physician: I would have you but open your hearts to receive Me, and I will open heaven to receive you, but you will rather stay with your sins and die, than come to Me and live, "Israel would none of Me" (Psalm 81:11). Well, sinners, I will weep at your funerals. ...The men of the world see not the beauty of Christ. He doth not want worth but they want eyes. O unhappy man (saith Austin) who knowest all things else but Christ! thy knowledge will but serve to light thee to hell.

But are you healed? Then break forth into thankfulness. "Let the high praises of God be in their mouth" (Psalm 149:6). God expects thankfulness. "Were there not ten cleansed? but where are the nine? There are not found that returned to give glory to God, save this stranger" (Luke 17:17-18.)

3.
Giving

"He that giveth unto the poor shall not lack."

PROVERBS 28:27

"Give, and it shall be given unto you."—LUKE 6:38

Faith alone justifies, but justifying faith is not alone. Good works though they are not the *causes* of salvation, yet they are the *evidences*. Faith must not be built upon works, but works must be built upon faith. Faith doth *justify* works; works do *testify* faith. "I will shew thee my faith by my works" (James 2:18).

"If a brother or sister be naked, and destitute of daily food, and one of you say unto them, Depart in peace, be ye warmed and filled: notwithstanding ye give them not those things which are needful to the body; what doth it profit?" (James 2:15-16). There are some who perhaps will give the poor good words, and that is all. Good words are but a cold kind of charity. Let your words be as smooth as oil, they will not heal the wounded, let them drop as the honeycomb, they will not feed the hungry. "Though I speak with the tongues of men and of angels, and have not charity, I am become as sounding brass, or a

GIVING

tinkling cymbal" (1 Corinthians 13:1). 'Tis better to be charitable as a saint than eloquent as an angel.

"He shall have judgment without mercy, that hath shewed no mercy" (James 2:13). Dives denied Lazarus a crumb of bread, and Dives was denied a drop of water.

"I was an hungred, and ye gave Me no meat: I was thirsty, and ye gave Me no drink" (Matthew 25:42). Christ doth not say ye took away My meat, but ye gave Me none.

Remember that excellent saying of St. Austin, "Give those things to the poor which you cannot keep, that you may receive those things which you cannot lose."

The way to lay up, is to lay out. Other parts of your estate you leave behind, but that which is given to Christ's poor is hoarded up in heaven. That is a blessed kind of giving, which, though it makes the purse the lighter, makes the crown the heavier. You shall have good security; "he that hath pity upon the poor, lendeth unto the LORD; and that which he hath given will He pay him again" (Proverbs 19:17). You shall be paid with over-plus. For a *wedge of gold* which you have parted with, you shall have a *weight of glory*. For a cup of cold water you shall have rivers of pleasure which run at God's right hand for evermore. The interest comes to infinitely more than the principal.

Your charity must be free. "Thou shalt surely give ... and thy heart shall not be grieved" (Deuteronomy 15:10). That is, thou shalt not be troubled at parting with thy money; he that gives *grievingly*, gives *grudgingly*. Charity must flow like spring water. The heart must be the spring, the hand the pipe, the poor the cistern. God loves a cheerful giver.

We must give that which is our own (Isaiah 58:7). "To deal thy bread to the hungry", it must be bread of thy

25

own, "For I the Lord love judgment, I hate robbery for burnt offering."

Do all *in* Christ. Out of Christ all our alms-deeds are but the fruit of the wild olive. They are not good works but dead works.

Do all *for* Christ. As Mary did out of love bring her ointments and sweet spices to anoint Christ's dead body: so out of love to Christ bring your ointments and anoint His living body, His saints and members.

Works of mercy are to be done in humility. Pride will be creeping into our best things; beware of this dead fly in the box of ointment. As the silkworm when she weaves her curious works, hides herself within the silk, so we should hide ourselves from pride and vanity.

The saints are brought in at last as disowning their works of charity. "Lord, when saw we Thee an hungred and fed Thee? or thirsty and gave Thee drink?" (Matthew 25:37). A good Christian doth not only empty his hand of alms, but empties his heart of pride; while he raiseth up the poor out of the dust, he lays himself in the dust.

Distribute your silver and gold to the poor before "the silver cord be loosed, or the golden bowl be broken" (Ecclesiastes 12:6). Make your hands your executors, not as some do who reserve all they give till the term of life is ready to expire. And truly what is then bestowed, is not given away, but taken away by death. 'Tis not charity but necessity. Be not like the medlar which is never good till it be rotten.

4.
Longing

"He satisfieth the longing soul, and filleth the hungry soul with goodness."—Psalm 107:9

"Blessed are they which do hunger and thirst after righteousness: for they shall be filled" (Matthew 5:6). Though thou hast not so much righteousness as thou wouldst, yet thou art blessed, because thou hungerest after it; desire is the best discovery of a Christian, actions may be counterfeit; a man may do a good action for a bad end. So did Jehu. Actions may be compulsory: a man may be forced to do that which is good, but not to *will* that which is good. These hungerings after righteousness proceed from love; a man doth not desire that which he doth not love; if thou didst not love Christ, thou couldst not hunger after Him.

The hypocrite doth not so much desire the way of righteousness as the crown of righteousness: his desire is not to be made like Christ, but to reign with Christ. This was Balaam's desire, "Let me die the death of the righteous" (Numbers 23:10). This is the hypocrite's hunger; a child of God desires Christ for Himself. To a believer, not only heaven is precious, but Christ is precious (1 Peter 2:7).

Hypocrites' desires are but desires, they are lazy and sluggish. "The desire of the slothful killeth him; for his hands refuse to labour" (Proverbs 21:25). But true desire is quickened into endeavour, "With my soul have I *desired* Thee in the night; yea, with my spirit within me will I *seek* Thee early" (Isaiah 26:9).

If we do not thirst here we shall thirst when it is too late; if we do not thirst as David did, "My soul thirsteth for God" (Psalm 42:2), we shall thirst as Dives did for a drop of water.

"They shall be filled." God never bids us seek Him in vain. "He hath filled the hungry with good things" (Luke 1:53). "He satisfieth the longing soul" (Psalm 107:9). God will not let us lose our longing.

A man may hunger after the world and not be filled; the world is fading, not filling. A man may be filled and not satisfied. A sinner may take his fill of sin, but it is far from satisfaction, "The backslider in heart shall be filled with his own ways" (Proverbs 14:14). This is such a filling as the damned in hell have, they shall be full of the fury of the Lord; but he that hungers after righteousness shall be satisfyingly filled. "My people shall be satisfied with My goodness" (Jeremiah 31:14).

God can fill the hungry soul. "With Thee is the fountain of life" (Psalm 36:9). The cistern may be empty and cannot fill us. But the fountain is filling. The fulness of God is an infinite fulness, it knows neither bounds nor bottom. It is a constant fulness, "Thou art the same" (Psalm 102:27). God can never be exhausted, His fulness is overflowing and ever-flowing.

God fills the hungry soul out of His tender compassion. When the multitude had nothing to eat, Christ was moved with compassion. Let the hungry soul think this, though I am full of wants, yet my God is full of bowels.

God will fill the hungry that He may fulfil His word. "Blessed are ye that hunger now: for *ye shall be filled*" (Luke 6:21). Hath the Lord spoken and shall it not come to pass? As "His compassions fail not" (Lamentations 3:22), so He will not suffer His "faithfulness to fail" (Psalm 89:33). If the hungry soul should not be filled, the promise should not be fulfilled.

God will fill the hungry because He Himself hath stirred up the hunger. As in case of prayer, when God prepares the heart to pray, He prepares His ear to hear (Psalm 10:17). So in the case of spiritual hunger, when God prepares the heart to hunger, He will prepare His hand to fill.

God keeps open house for hungry sinners (Isaiah 55:1-2).

There is no such thing as blind fate, but there is a Providence that guides and governs the world. "The lot is cast into the lap, but the whole disposing thereof is of the LORD" (Proverbs 16:33). ... Providence is God's ordering all issues and events of things, after the counsel of His will, to His own glory. ... The wheels in a clock seem to move contrary one to the other, but they help forward the motion of the clock, and make the alarum strike; so the providences of God seem to be cross wheels; but for all that they shall carry on the good of the elect. ... God is not like an artificer that builds a house, and then leaves it, but like a pilot He steers the ship of the whole creation.

"The eye of the LORD is upon them that fear Him, upon them that hope in His mercy; to deliver their soul from death, and to keep them alive in famine" (Psalm 33:18-19). God by His providential care shields off dangers from His people, and sets a lifeguard of angels about them

(Psalm 34:7). God's providence keeps the very bones of the saints (Psalm 34:20). It bottles their tears (Psalm 56:8). It strengthens the saints in their weakness (Hebrews 11:34). It supplies all their wants out of its alms-basket (Psalm 23:5). "Verily thou shalt be fed" (Psalm 37:3). If God will give His people a kingdom when they die, He will not deny them daily bread while they live.

God, who bounds everything else, is Himself without bounds. He sets bounds to the sea; *Huc usque*[1]; "Hitherto shalt thou come, and no further"; He sets bounds to the angels; they, like the cherubims, move and stand at His appointment (Ezekiel 10:16), but He is infinite without bounds. He who can span the heavens, and weigh the earth in scales, must needs be infinite (Isaiah 40:22). "Do not I fill heaven and earth?" (Jeremiah 23:24). The humble heart is His throne, in regard to His gracious presence (Isaiah 57:15); and heaven is His throne, in regard to His glorious presence (Isaiah 66:1); and yet neither of these thrones will hold Him, for the heaven of heavens cannot contain Him.

---

[1] Thus far

5.
Contentment

"I have learned, in whatsoever state I am, therewith to be content."—PHILIPPIANS 4:11

"I have learned." The Apostle doth not say, "I have heard, that in every estate I should be content", but, "I have learned." It is not enough for Christians to hear their duty, but they must learn their duty. It is one thing to hear, and another thing to learn; as it is one thing to eat, and another thing to digest food. Christians hear much, but, it is to be feared, learn little.

If your estate be small, yet God can bless a little. It is not how much money we have, but how much blessing. He that often curses the bags of gold, can bless the meal in the barrel, and the oil in the cruse. What if thou hast not the full flesh-pots? yet thou hast a promise, I will "bless her provision" (Psalm 132:15), and then a little goes a great way. Be content, that thou hast the dew of a blessing distilled: a dinner of green herbs, where love is, is sweet; I may add, where the love of God is. Another may have more estate than you, but more care; more riches, less rest; more revenues, but withal more occasions of expense: he hath a greater inheritance, yet perhaps God doth not give

31

him "power to eat thereof" (Ecclesiastes 6:2); he holds more, but enjoys less; in a word, thou hast less gold then he, perhaps less guilt.

Discontent keeps a man from enjoying what he doth possess. A drop or two of vinegar will sour a whole glass of wine. Comfort depends upon contentment. It is not trouble that troubles, but discontent; it is not the water without the ship, but the water that gets within the leak which sinks it; it is not outward afflictions that can make the life of a Christian sad; a contented mind would sail above these waters; but when there is a leak of discontent open, and trouble gets into the heart, then it is disquieted and sinks.

The discontented person thinks everything he doth for God too much, and everything God doth for him too little.

There are no sins God's people are more subject to than unbelief and impatience; they are ready, either to faint through unbelief, or to fret through impatience. When men fly out against God by discontent and impatience, it is a sign they do not believe "that all things work together for good, to them that love God." Discontent is an ungrateful sin, because we have more mercies than afflictions; and it is an irrational sin, because afflictions work for good. Discontent is a sin which puts us upon sin. "Fret not thyself to do evil" (Psalm 37:8). He that frets will be ready to do evil: fretting Jonah was sinning (Jonah 4:9). The devil blows the coals of passion and discontent, and then warms himself at the fire.

"All things work together for good to them that love God." Shall we be discontented at that which works for our good? If one friend should throw a bag of money at another, and in throwing it, should graze his head, he would not be troubled much, seeing by this means he had got a bag of money. So the Lord may bruise us by afflictions, but it is to enrich us; these afflictions work for us a weight of glory; and shall we be discontented?

Immoderate care takes the heart off from better things; and usually while we are thinking how we shall do to live, we forget how to die. We may sooner by our care add a furlong to our grief, than a foot to our comfort.

Remember thou art to be here but a day; thou hast but a short way to go, and what need a long provision for a short way? If a traveller hath but enough to bring him to his journey's end, he desires no more.

How hard it is for a rich man to enter into the kingdom of heaven! (Luke 18:24). His golden weights keep him from ascending up the hill of God. Be content then with a little; if you have but enough to pay for your passage to heaven, it sufficeth.

Humility is like the lead to the net, which keeps the soul down when it is rising through passion; and contentment is like the cork, which keeps the heart up when it is sinking through discouragement.

Is not many a man contented to suffer reproach for maintaining his lust? and shall not we for maintaining the truth? Some glory in that which is their shame (Philippians 3:19); and shall we be ashamed of that which is our glory?

What need he complain of the world's emptiness that hath God's fulness? "The LORD is the portion of mine inheritance", saith David (Psalm 16:5); then let the lines fall where they will, in a sick bed, or prison, I will say, "The lines are fallen unto me in pleasant places; yea, I have a goodly heritage."

"The God which fed me all my life long unto this day" (Genesis 48:15). Hath not God provided liberally for you. Thou never feedest, but mercy carves for thee; thou never goest to bed, but mercy draws the curtains, and sets a guard of angels about thee.

"The LORD is good to all" (Psalm 145:9). Sweet dewdrops are on the thistle, as well as on the rose. God's mercy is *free*. To set up merit is to destroy mercy. Nothing can deserve mercy, nor force it. We may force God to punish us, but not to love us. "I will love them freely" (Hosea 14:4). Every link in the chain of salvation is wrought and interwoven with free grace. Election is free. "He hath chosen us in Him … according to the good pleasure of His will" (Ephesians 1:4-5). Justification is free, "Being justified freely by His grace" (Romans 3:24). Salvation is free, "According to His mercy He saved us" (Titus 3:5). Say not then, I am unworthy; for mercy is free. If God should show mercy to such only as are worthy, He would show none at all. … God's mercy is an overflowing mercy; it is infinite: "Plenteous in mercy" (Psalm 86:5). "Rich in mercy" (Ephesians 2:4). "Multitude of Thy tender mercies" (Psalm 51:1). The vial of wrath drops, but the fountain of mercy runs. … God has morning mercies, His mercies "are new every morning" (Lamentations 3:23). He has night mercies, "In the night His song shall be with me" (Psalm 42:8). God's mercy is eternal, "The mercy of the LORD is from everlasting to everlasting" (Psalm 103:17). As His mercy is overflowing so it is everflowing.

Doth God give us a Christ, and will He deny us a crust? If God doth not give us what we crave, He will give us what we need.

Prosperity often deafens the ear against God. "I spake to thee in thy prosperity, but thou saidst, I will not hear"

(Jeremiah 22:21). Soft pleasures harden the heart. Prosperity has its honey, and also its sting. Anxious care is the evil spirit that haunts the rich man; when his chests are full of money, his heart is full of care. Sunshine is pleasant, but sometimes it scorches. The spreading of a full table may be the spreading of a snare. Many have been sunk to hell with golden weights. "They that will be rich fall into many hurtful lusts, which drown men in perdition" (1 Timothy 6:9). The world's golden sands are quicksands. What if we have less food we have less snare; if less dignity, less danger. As we lack the rich provisions of the world, so we lack the temptations. To give us Christ is more than if God had given us all the world. He can make more worlds, but He has no more Christs to bestow. If you have but daily bread enough to suffice nature, be content. Consider it is not having abundance that always makes life comfortable. A staff may help the traveller, but a bundle of staves will be a burden to him. The world is but a great inn. If God give you sufficient to pay for your charges in your inn, you may be content, you shall have enough when you come to your own country.

"What time I am afraid, I will trust in Thee" (Psalm 56:3). Faith cures the trembling in heart; it gets above fear as oil swims above the water. To trust in God makes Him to be a God to us. God will turn all evils to our good (Romans 8:28). Joseph's imprisonment was a means for his advancement. Out of the bitterest drug He will distil His glory and our salvation. In short, He will be our guide to death, our comfort in death, and our reward after death. "Happy is that people, whose God is the LORD" (Psalm 144:15).

6.
Poverty

"Blessed are the poor in spirit: for theirs is the Kingdom of Heaven."—MATTHEW 5:3

Some think if they can fill their bags with gold, then they are rich; but they who are poor in spirit are the rich men; this poverty entitles them to a kingdom. How poor are they that think themselves rich! How rich are they that see themselves poor. There are some paradoxes in religion that the world cannot understand; for a man to become a fool that he may be wise (1 Corinthians 3:18), to save his life by losing it (Matthew 16:25), and being poor to be rich, reason laughs at; but "blessed are the poor, for theirs is the kingdom"; under these rags is hid cloth of gold.

"Blessed are the poor in spirit." This poverty is your riches; you may have the world's riches, and yet be poor; you cannot have this poverty, but you must be rich; poverty of spirit entitles you to Christ's riches.

Blessedness doth not lie in the acquisition of worldly things. Christ doth not say, Blessed are the rich, or blessed are the noble; yet too many idolize these things: Man by the fall hath not only lost his crown, but his head-piece. The tree of blessedness doth not grow in an earthly paradise. Hath not God cursed the ground for sin? Yet many are digging for felicity here, as if they would fetch a blessing out of a curse.

That which cannot quiet the heart in a storm, cannot entitle a man to blessedness; earthly things accumulated, cannot rock the troubled heart quiet, therefore cannot make one blessed. When Saul was sore distressed, could all the jewels of his crown comfort him? "They shall cast their silver in the streets ... their silver and their gold shall not be able to deliver them in the day of the wrath of the LORD" (Ezekiel 7:19).

That which is but for a season cannot make one blessed; all things under the sun are but for a season. "The world passeth away" (1 John 2:17). Riches and honour are fugitive: while they are with us they are going away from us, like ice, which melts away while it is in your hand.

Things which do more vex than comfort, cannot make a man blessed; but such are all things under the sun. As riches are compared to "wind" to show their vanity (Hosea 12:1), so to "thorns", to show their vexation (Matthew 13:22). Thorns are not more apt to tear our garments, than riches are to tear our hearts; they are thorns in the gathering, they prick with care; and as they pierce the hand with care of getting, so they wound the heart with fear of losing.

Those things which (if we have nothing else) will make us cursed, cannot make us blessed. "They that will be rich fall into temptation, and a snare, and into many foolish and hurtful lusts, which drown men in destruction and perdition" (1 Timothy 6:9). How many have pulled down their souls to build up an estate! A ship may be so laden with gold that it sinks; many a man's gold hath sunk him to hell. The rich sinner seals up money in his bag, and

God seals up a curse with it. "Woe to him … that ladeth himself with thick clay" (Habakkuk 2:6).

To such as are cut short in their allowance, whose cup doth not overflow, but their tears; be not too much troubled; remember these outward comforts cannot make you blessed; you might live rich and die cursed; you might treasure up an estate, and God might treasure up wrath; be not perplexed about these things; the want whereof cannot make you miserable, nor the enjoyment make you blessed.

Earthly riches, saith Austin, are full of poverty. They cannot enrich the soul; oftentimes under silken apparel, there is a threadbare soul.

The common mercies wicked men have, are not loadstones to draw them nearer to God, but millstones to sink them deeper in hell (1 Timothy 6:9). Their delicious dainties are like Haman's banquet; after all their lordly fare, death will bring in the reckoning, and they must pay it in hell.

You never knew a man surfeit himself upon the world, and sick of love to Christ; while Israel fed with delight upon garlic and onions, they never hungered after manna. The love of earthly things will quench the desire of spiritual. "Love not the world" (1 John 2:15); the sin is not in the having but the loving.

Godly and earthly is a contradiction. "For many walk, of whom I now tell you, even weeping, that they are the enemies of the cross of Christ, whose god is their belly, who mind earthly things" (Philippians 3:18-19). We read the earth swallowed up Korah alive (Numbers 16:32). This judgment is on many, the earth swallows up their time, and thoughts, and discourse, they are buried twice; their hearts are buried in the earth before their bodies.

God allows us the use of the world (1 Timothy 6:7), but take heed of the love of it; he that is in love with the world will be out of love with the cross. "Demas hath forsaken me, having loved this present world" (2 Timothy 4:10). Before a man can die for Christ he must be dead to the world. It will be an easy thing to die, when we are dead before in our affections.

How soon we are broken upon the soft pillow of ease! Adam in paradise was overcome, when Job on the dunghill was a conqueror.

"I cannot be poor," saith Bernard, "as long as God is rich, for His riches are mine." Whatever we lose for God, we shall find again in Him. "We have left all," say the disciples, "and have followed Thee" (Mark 10:28). Alas! what had they left? A few sorry boats and tackling! They parted with movable goods for the unchangeable God. All losses are made up in Him: we may be losers *for* God, we shall not be losers *by* Him.

"Thou hast put gladness in my heart" (Psalm 4:7). Worldly joys put gladness into the face. The rich Corinthians "glory in appearance and not in heart" (2 Corinthians 5:12); but the Spirit of God puts gladness into the heart; divine joys are heart joys: "Their heart shall rejoice in the LORD" (Zechariah 10:7); "Your heart shall rejoice" (John 16:22).

Christ, who had all riches, scorned earthly riches; He was born poor, the manger was His cradle, the cobwebs His curtains: He lived poor, He had not where to lay His head: He died poor, He had no crown-lands, only His coat was left, and that the soldiers parted among them:

and His funeral was suitable, for as He was born in another man's house, so He was buried in another man's tomb.

"For ye know the grace of our Lord Jesus Christ, that, though He was rich, yet for your sakes He became poor" (2 Corinthians 8:9). He could have brought down a house from heaven with Him, or have challenged the high places of the earth; but He was contented to live poor that we might die rich: the manger was His cradle. He, who is now preparing mansions for us in heaven, had none for Himself on earth; He had not where to lay His head.

He was poor, that He might make us rich. He was born of a virgin, that we might be born of God. He took our flesh, that might give us His Spirit. He lay in the manger that we might lie in paradise. He came down from heaven that He might bring us to heaven.

7.
Afflictions

"It is good for me that I have been afflicted."—PSALM 119:71

Afflictions quicken our pace in the way to heaven; it is with us, as with children sent on an errand, if they meet with apples or flowers by the way, they linger and make no great haste home, but if anything fright them, then they run with all the speed they can to their father's house: so, in prosperity, we are gathering the apples and flowers, and do not much mind heaven, but if troubles begin to arise, and the times grow frightful, then we make more haste to heaven, and with David, "run the way of God's commandments" (Psalm 119:32).

God's people have no writ of ease granted them, no charter of exemption from trouble in this life. While the wicked are kept in sugar, the godly are often kept in brine. God lets His people be in the house of bondage for probation or trial. "Who led thee through that great and terrible wilderness, ... that He might humble thee, and that He might prove thee" (Deuteronomy 8:15-16). Affliction is the touch-stone of sincerity. "Thou, O God, hast proved us; Thou hast tried us, as silver is tried; ... Thou laidst affliction upon our loins" (Psalm 66:10-11).

Hypocrites may embrace the true religion in prosperity, but he is a good Christian who will keep close to God in a time of suffering. "All this is come upon us, yet have we not forgotten Thee" (Psalm 44:17).

The stones which are cut out for a building are first hewn and squared. The godly are called "living stones" (1 Peter 2:5). God first hews and polishes them by affliction, that they may be fit for the heavenly building. The house of bondage prepares for the house not made with hands.

Afflictions on the godly make them better, but afflictions on the wicked make them worse. The godly pray more (Psalm 130:1). The wicked blaspheme more. "Men were scorched with great heat, and blasphemed the name of God" (Revelation 16:9). Afflictions on the wicked make them more impenitent; every plague upon Egypt increased the plague of hardness in Pharaoh's heart. Affliction of the godly is like bruising spices, which are most sweet and fragrant: affliction on the wicked is like pounding weeds with a pestle, which makes them more unsavoury.

A sick bed often teaches more than a sermon; we can best see the ugly visage of sin in the glass of affliction.

What if we have more of the rough file, if we have less rust! Afflictions carry away nothing but the dross of sin.

When affliction or death comes to a wicked man, it takes away his soul; when it comes to a godly man it only takes away his sin. ... "We are chastened of the Lord, that we should not be condemned with the world" (1 Corinthians 11:32). He works out sin and works in grace.

"I will be with him in trouble" (Psalm 91:15). When we are most assaulted, we shall be most assisted. What if we have more trouble than others, if we have more of God with us than others? It cannot be ill with that man with whom God is. Better to be in prison and have God's presence, than be in a palace without it.

It is one heart-quieting consideration, in all the afflictions that befall us, that God hath a special hand in them: "The Almighty hath afflicted me" (Ruth 1:21). Instruments can no more stir till God gives them a commission, than the axe can cut of itself without a hand. Job eyed God in his affliction: therefore, as Augustine observes, he doth not say, "The Lord gave, and the devil took away", but "The Lord hath taken away." Whoever brings an affliction to us, it is God that sends it. Afflictions work for good. "It is good for me that I have been afflicted" (Psalm 119:71). Joseph's brethren throw him into a pit; afterwards they sell him; then he is cast into prison; yet all this did work for his good: his abasement made way for his advancement; he was made the second man in the kingdom. "Ye thought evil against me, but God meant it unto good" (Genesis 50:20). Jacob wrestled with the angel, and the hollow of Jacob's thigh was out of joint; this was sad; but God turned it to good, for there he saw God's face, and there the Lord blessed him. "Jacob called the name of the place Peniel, for I have seen God face to face" (Genesis 32:30). Who would not be willing to have a bone out of joint, so that he might have a sight of God? King Manasseh was bound in chains, this was sad to see — a crown of gold changed into fetters; but it wrought for his good, for, "When he was in affliction he besought the LORD, and humbled himself greatly, and the LORD was intreated of him" (2 Chronicles 33:12-13). He was more beholden to his iron chain, than to his golden crown; the one made him proud, the other made him humble. Paul was smitten with blindness; this was uncomfortable, but it turned to his good; God did by that blindness make way for the light of grace to shine into his soul.

God sweetens outward pain with inward peace. "Your sorrow shall be turned into joy" (John 16:20). God's rod has honey at the end of it.

David saith, "My times are in Thy hand" (Psalm 31:15). If our times were in our own hand, we would have deliverance too soon; if they were in our enemy's hand, we should have deliverance too late; but my times are in Thy hand; and God's time is ever best. Everything is beautiful in its season: when the mercy is ripe, we shall have it. It is true we are now between the hammer and the anvil; but do not cast away your anchor; God sees when the mercy will be in season. When His people are low enough, and the enemy high enough, then appears the Church's morning-star: Let God alone to His time. "My soul waiteth for the Lord" (Psalm 130:6). Good reason God should have the timing of our mercies, "I the Lord will hasten it in His time." Deliverance may tarry beyond our time; but it will not tarry beyond God's time. ... After a wet night of affliction, comes a bright morning of the resurrection: if our lives are short, our trials cannot be long. ... Time is short (1 Corinthians 7:29). Though the cross be heavy, we have but a little way to carry it. The time being short the waiting time cannot be long.

When the hearts of His people are most humble, when their prayers are most fervent, when their faith is strongest, when their forces are weakest, when their enemies are highest; then is the usual time that Christ puts forth His kingly power for their deliverance (Isaiah 33:2, 8-10).

Afflictions work for good, as they conform us to Christ. His life was a series of sufferings, "a man of sorrows, and acquainted with grief" (Isaiah 53:3). He wept, and bled. Was His head crowned with thorns, and do we think to be crowned with roses? It is good to be like Christ, though it be by sufferings.

"Let none of you suffer ... as an evil doer" (1 Peter 4:15). I am not of Cyprian's mind, that the thief on the cross suffered as a martyr; no, he suffered as an evil doer; Christ indeed took pity on him, and saved him; he died a saint, but not a martyr. When men suffer by the hand of a magistrate, these do not suffer persecution, but execution: they die not as martyrs, but as malefactors; they suffer evil for being evil.

God loves a thankful Christian. Job thanked God when He took all away: "The LORD hath taken away, blessed be the name of the LORD" (Job 1:21). Many will thank God when He gives, Job thanks Him when He takes away, because he knew God would work good out of it. We read of saints with harps in their hands (Revelation 14:2), an emblem of praise. We meet many Christians who have tears in their eyes, and complaints in their mouths; but there are few with their harps in their hands, who praise God in affliction. Every bird can sing in spring, but some birds will sing in the dead of winter. A good Christian will bless God, not only at the sun-rising, but at the sun-setting. Well may we, in the worst that befalls us, have a psalm of thankfulness, because all things work for good. If God makes all things turn to our good, how right is it that we should make all things tend to His glory! "Do all to the glory of God" (1 Corinthians 10:31).

"His mercies are new every morning" (Lamentations 3:23). Mercy comes in as constantly as the tide; nay, how many tides of mercy do we see in one day. We never feed, but mercy carves every bit to us; we never drink but in the golden cup of mercy; we never go abroad, but mercy sets a guard of angels about us; we never lie down in bed, but mercy draws the curtains of protection close about us. Shall we receive so many good things at the hand of God, and shall we not receive evil? Our mercies far outweigh our afflictions; for one affliction we have a thousand mercies. The sea of God's mercy would swallow up a few drops of affliction.

Many, to rid themselves out of trouble, run themselves into sin. When God has bound them with the cords of affliction, they go to the devil to loosen their bands. Better it is to stay in affliction than to sin ourselves out of it.

Affliction quickens the spirit of prayer; Jonah was asleep in the ship, but at prayer in the whale's belly. Perhaps in a time of health and prosperity we pray in a cold and formal manner, we put no coals to the incense, we scarcely minded our own prayers, and how should God mind them? God sends some cross or other to make us take hold of Him. "They poured out a prayer, when Thy chastening hand was upon them" (Isaiah 26:16); now their prayer pierced the heavens. In times of trouble we pray feelingly, and we never pray so fervently as when we pray feelingly.

When God puts His children to the school of the cross, He deals with them tenderly, because He does not leave them without a promise, "God is faithful, who will not suffer you to be tempted above that ye are able." He will not lay a giant's burden upon a child's back, nor will He stretch the strings of the instrument too much, lest they should break. If God sees it good to strike with one hand, He will support with the other; either He will make the faith stronger, or render the yoke lighter.

God loves His people when He is giving the bitter diet-drink of affliction. God's rod and God's love, they both stand together. It is no love in God to let men go on in sin, and never smite. God's greatest curse is when He afflicts not for sin. Let us feel God's hand so that we may have His heart.

Afflictions add to the saints' glory. The more the diamond is cut, the more it sparkles; the heavier the saints' cross is, the heavier shall be their crown.

If God be our God, He will give us peace in trouble. When there is a storm without, He will make peace within. The world can create trouble in peace, but God can create peace in trouble.

8.
Persecution

"Blessed are they which are persecuted for righteousness' sake: for theirs is the kingdom of heaven."—MATTHEW 5:10

Affliction is the beaten road in which all the saints have gone. The living stones in the spiritual building have been all hewn and polished. Christ's lily has grown among the thorns. "All that will live godly in Christ Jesus, shall suffer persecution" (2 Timothy 3:12).

"We must through much tribulation enter into the kingdom of God" (Acts 14:22). Though Christ died to take away the curse from us, yet not to take away the cross. The way to heaven, though it be full of roses in regard of the comforts of the Holy Ghost, yet it is full of thorns in regard to persecutions. It is a saying of Ambrose, there is no Abel but hath his Cain. Put the cross in your creed.

A true saint carries Christ in his heart, and the cross on his shoulders. Christ's kingdom on earth is the kingdom of the cross. Christ and His cross are never parted. Persecution is the legacy bequeathed by Christ to His people. "In the world ye shall have tribulation" (John 16:33). We are all for reigning. "When wilt thou restore the Kingdom again to Israel?" But the Apostle tells us of suffering before reigning. "If we suffer we shall also reign with Him" (2 Timothy 2:12). Was His head crowned with thorns, and do we think to be crowned with roses?

Let us take heed of becoming persecutors: some think there is no persecution but fire and sword; yes, there is persecution of the tongue. ... Reviling is called persecution, "men shall revile you and persecute you"; this is tongue persecution. "His words were softer than oil, yet were they drawn swords" (Psalm 55:21). You may kill a man as well in his name as in his person; a good name is as precious ointment. Now to smite another in his name, is by our Saviour called persecution. Thus the primitive saints endured the persecution of the tongue. They "had trial of cruel mockings" (Hebrews 11:36). Slandering is tongue persecution, "When men shall revile you, and persecute you, and shall say all manner of evil against you falsely." Thus Paul was slandered in his doctrine; it was reported he should preach, men might do evil that good might come of it. Thus Christ, who did cast out devils, was charged to have a devil (John 8:48). "They laid to My charge things that I knew not" (Psalm 35:11).

WHY THERE MUST BE PERSECUTION

First, it is God's decree, "We are appointed thereunto" (1 Thessalonians 3:3). Whoever brings the suffering, God sends it. God did bid Shimei curse; Shimei's tongue was the arrow, but it was God that did shoot it. Second, it is God's design for the trial of His saints. "Many shall be tried." It discovers true saints from hypocrites; unsound hearts pretend fair in prosperity, but in a time of persecution fall away (Matthew 13:20-21). Hypocrites will follow Christ to Mount Olivet, but not to Mount Calvary. Suffering times are sifting times. "When He hath tried me, I shall come forth as gold" (Job 23:10). God lets His children be in the furnace that they may be "partakers of

His holiness" (Hebrews 12:10). "I am black but comely" (Canticles [Song of Songs] 1:5). The torrid zone of persecution made the spouse's skin black, but her soul fair.

"Blessed are they which are persecuted." What is that suffering which will make us blessed?

When we suffer in a good cause. Blessed are they which suffer "for righteousness' sake". It is the cause that makes a martyr. "For the hope of Israel I am bound with this chain" (Acts 28:20).

When we suffer with a good conscience. A man may have a good cause, and a bad conscience. Saint Paul, as he had a just cause, so he had a pure conscience. "I have lived in all good conscience before God until this day" (Acts 23:1). A good conscience will make a man suffer with comfort.

When we have a good call. When "ye shall be brought before governors and kings" (Matthew 10:18). If God by His providence open a door, a man may fly in time of persecution (Matthew 10:23). But when he is brought before kings, and the case is such that either he must suffer, or the truth must suffer; here is a clear call to suffering.

When we have good ends in our suffering. "When ye shall be brought before governors and kings for *My sake*." The primitive Christians did burn more in love than in fire; when we look at God in our sufferings, and are willing to make His crown flourish, though it be in our ashes, this is that suffering which carries away the garland of glory.

When we suffer as Christians. "If any man suffer as a Christian, let him not be ashamed" (1 Peter 4:16).

When we suffer with patience. "Take, my brethren, the prophets … for an example of suffering affliction, and of patience" (James 5:10).

PERSECUTION

When we suffer with cheerfulness. Thus Moses suffered cheerfully. Moses, when he was come to years, chose rather "to suffer affliction with the people of God, than to enjoy the pleasures of sin for a season" (Hebrews 11:25). "He chose to suffer affliction", suffering was not so much his choice; the cross was not so much imposed as embraced. "They departed from the presence of the council, *rejoicing* that they were counted worthy to suffer shame for His name." They rejoiced that they were so far graced, as to be disgraced for the name of Christ. Christ's marks in Saint Paul's body were prints of glory.

When we suffer and *pray*. "Pray for them which despitefully use you, and persecute you." Stephen prayed for his persecutors, "Lord, lay not this sin to their charge." Austin saith, the Church of God was beholden to Stephen's prayer for all that benefit which was reaped by Paul's ministry.

GOD WITH US IN TROUBLE

"I will be with him in trouble" (Psalm 91:15). What if we have more afflictions than others, if we have more of God's company! "I will deliver him and honour him" (Psalm 91:15). He who can strengthen our faith, can break our fetters. "Your sorrow shall be turned into joy" (John 16:20). There is the water turned into wine. "Be of good cheer, Paul." In time of persecution God broacheth the wine of consolation; cordials are kept for fainting.

CHRIST HAS BEEN BEFORE IN SUFFERING

Consider what Christ endured for us. Christ's whole life was a series of sufferings: Christian, what is thy suffering? Art thou poor? So was Christ: "The Son of Man hath not where to lay His head" (Matthew 8:20). Art thou surrounded with enemies? So was Christ: "Against Thy holy Servant Jesus ... both Herod, and Pontius Pilate, with the

Gentiles, and the people of Israel, were gathered together" (Acts 4:27). Do our enemies lay claim to religion? So did His: "And the chief priests took the silver pieces, and said, It is not lawful for to put them into the treasury, because it is the price of blood" (Matthew 27:6). Godly persecutors! Art thou reproached? So was Christ: "The reproaches of them that reproached thee are fallen upon Me" (Psalm 69:9). Art thou slandered? So was Christ: "The Pharisees said, He casteth out devils through the prince of the devils" (Matthew 9:34). Art thou ignominiously used? So was Christ: "Some began to spit on Him, and to cover His face and to buffet Him, and say unto Him, Prophesy: and the servants did strike Him with the palms of their hands" (Mark 14:65). Art thou betrayed by friends? So was Christ: "Jesus said unto him, Judas, betrayest thou the Son of Man with a kiss?" (Luke 22:48). Is thy estate sequestered? And do the wicked cast lots for it? So Christ was dealt with: "They parted My garments among them, and upon My vesture did they cast lots" (Matthew 27:35). Do we suffer unjustly? So did Christ: His very judge did acquit Him: "Then said Pilate to the chief priests and to the people, I find no fault in this man" (Luke 23:4). Art thou barbarously dragged and haled away to suffering? So was Christ: "And when they had bound Him, they led Him away" (Matthew 27:2). Dost thou suffer death? So did Christ: "And when they were come to the place, which is called Calvary, there they crucified Him" (Luke 23:33).

Did the Lord Jesus endure all this for us, and shall not we suffer persecution for His name? Our cup is nothing to the cup which Christ drank; His cup was mixed with the wrath of God; and if He did bear God's wrath for us, well may we bear man's wrath for Him.

PERSECUTION

SUFFERINGS ARE LIGHT

"Our light affliction" (2 Corinthians 4:17). It is heavy to flesh and blood, but it is light to faith. It is light in comparison of sin; he that feels sin heavy, feels suffering light. Affliction is light in comparison of hell; what is persecution to damnation? What is the fire of martyrdom to the fire of the damned? "Who knoweth the power of Thine anger?" (Psalm 90:11). Affliction is light in comparison with glory; the weight of glory makes persecution light.

SUFFERINGS ARE SHORT

"After that ye have suffered a while" (1 Peter 5:10), or as it is in the Greek, "a little". Our sufferings may be lasting, not everlasting. Persecution is *aspera*[1] but *brevis*[2]; though it hath a sting to torment, yet it hath a wing to fly. "Sorrow and sighing shall flee away" (Isaiah 35:10). It is but a while when the saints shall have a writ of ease granted them, they shall weep no more, suffer no more.

SUPPORT IN SUFFERING

While we suffer for Christ we suffer with Christ: "If so be that we suffer with Him" (Romans 8:17). Oh, saith the Christian, I shall never be able to hold out: but remember thou sufferest with Christ, He helps thee to suffer: "My grace is sufficient for thee" (2 Corinthians 12:9). "Underneath are the everlasting arms" (Deuteronomy 33:27). If Christ put the yoke of persecution over us, He will put His arms under us. The Lord Jesus will not only crown us when we conquer, but He will enable us to conquer.

[1] harsh, difficult, severe
[2] short-lived

Persecution and the love of God

They are blessed whom God loves, but persecution cannot hinder the love of God. "Who shall separate us from the love of Christ? shall tribulation, or distress, or persecution?" (Romans 8:35). The goldsmith loves his gold as well when it is in the fire, as when it is in his bag; God loves His children as well in adversity as in prosperity. "As many as I love, I rebuke and chasten" (Revelation 3:19). God sweetens their sufferings: "As the sufferings of Christ abound in us, so our consolation also aboundeth by Christ" (2 Corinthians 1:5). As the mother having given her child a bitter pill, gives it afterwards a lump of sugar.

The reward of suffering

"Great is your reward in heaven" (Matthew 5:12). A Christian may lose his life, but not his reward; he may lose his head, but not his crown. Not that we can merit this reward by our sufferings. "*I will give* thee a crown of life." The reward is the legacy which free-grace bequeaths. Alas! what proportion is there between a drop of blood, and a weight of glory? But though we have no reward by merit, we shall have it by grace; so it is in the text, "Great is your reward in heaven." Look upon the crown and faint if you can; the reward is as far above your thoughts, as it is beyond your deserts; a man that is to wade through a deep water, fixeth his eyes upon the firm land that is before him. While Christians are wading through the deep waters of persecution, they should fix the eyes of their faith on the land of promise; "Great is your reward in heaven." They that bear the cross patiently shall wear the crown triumphantly.

God brings us low before He raiseth us, as water is at the lowest ebb before there is a spring tide. When God would bring Israel to Canaan, a land flowing with milk and honey, He first led them through a sea and a wilderness. When He intended to advance Joseph to the second man in the kingdom, he cast him first into prison, and the iron entered into his soul. He usually lets it be darkest before the morning-star of deliverance appears.

Many desire to be glorified with Christ, but they are not content to suffer for Him. "If we suffer with Him, we shall also reign with Him" (2 Timothy 2:12). The wicked first reign and then suffer; the godly first suffer, and then reign.

Afflictions are safe guides to glory. The storm drives the ship into the harbour. Blessed storm that drives the soul into the heavenly harbour. Is it not better to go through affliction to glory, than through pleasure to misery?

9. Temptation

"Blessed is the man that endureth temptation: for when he is tried, he shall receive the crown of life, which the Lord hath promised to them that love Him."—JAMES 1:12

SATAN'S METHOD IN TEMPTING

He observes the temper and constitution. Satan will not tempt contrary to the natural disposition and temperament: he makes the wind and tide go together; that way the natural tide of the heart runs, that way the wind of temptation blows. Though the devil cannot know men's thoughts, yet he knows their temper, and accordingly he lays his baits.

Satan observes the fittest time to tempt in; as a cunning angler casts in his angle when the fish will bite best. Satan's time of tempting is usually after an ordinance. When we have been at solemn duties, we are apt to think all is done, and we grow remiss, and leave off that zeal and strictness as before; just as a soldier, who after a battle leaves off his armour, not once dreaming of an enemy. Satan watches his time, and, when we least suspect, then he throws in a temptation.

TEMPTATION

Satan makes use of near relations; the devil tempts by a proxy: thus he handed over a temptation to Job by his wife, "Dost thou still retain thine integrity?" (Job 2:9). A wife in the bosom may be the devil's instrument to tempt to sin.

Satan tempts to evil by them that are good; thus he gives poison in a golden cup. He tempted Christ by Peter. Peter dissuades Him from suffering. Master, pity Thyself. Who would have thought to have found the tempter in the mouth of an apostle?

Satan tempts to sin, under a pretence of religion. He is most to be feared when he transforms himself into an angel of light. He came to Christ with Scripture in his mouth: "It is written." The devil baits his hook with religion.

Peter was tempted to self-confidence, he presumed upon his own strength; and when he would needs stand alone, Christ let him fall: but this wrought for his good, it cost him many a tear. "He went out and wept bitterly" (Matthew 26:75). And now he grows more modest, he durst not say he loved Christ more than the other apostles. "Lovest thou Me more than these?" He durst not say so, his fall broke the neck of his pride.

Satan tempts to sin gradually: as the husbandman digs about the root of a tree, by degrees loosens it, and at last it falls. Satan steals by degrees into the heart; he is at first more plausible; he did not say to Eve at first, 'Eat the apple'; no, but he goes more subtilely to work; he puts forth a question, "Hath God said?" (Genesis 3:1); surely, Eve, thou art mistaken; the bountiful God never intended to debar thee one of the best trees of the garden. "Hath God said?" surely, either God did not say it; or, if He did, He never really intended it. Thus by degrees he wrought her to distrust, and then she took of the fruit and ate. O, take heed of Satan's first motions to sin, that seem more plausible. Oppose the beginnings of evil. He is first a fox and then a lion.

It is hard to climb up the hill of God with too many golden weights. Those that want the honours of the world, want the temptations of it. The world is a flattering enemy. The world doth never kiss us, but with an intent to betray us. "Love not the world" (1 John 2:15). The sin is not in the using of the world but in the loving. Living fish swim against the stream; so we must swim against the world, else we shall be carried down the stream, and fall into the Dead Sea.

"What I say unto you I say unto all, Watch" (Mark 13:37). We must ever keep sentinel. Sleep not upon your guard: our sleeping time is the devil's tempting time. When you have prayed against sin, watch against temptation.

Satan, in tempting, baits his hook with religion. He can hang out Christ's colours and tempt to sin under pretences of piety. Sometimes he is the white devil, and transforms himself into an angel of light. He wraps his poisonous pills in sugar.

Satan doth not tempt God's children because they have sin in them, but because they have grace in them. Had they no grace he would not disturb them, for where he keeps possession all is in peace (Luke 11:21). A thief will not assault an empty house, but where he thinks there is treasure. Though to be tempted is a trouble, yet to think why you are tempted is a comfort.

If you would not be overcome by temptation, flee the "occasions of sin". Occasions of sin have great force to

TEMPTATION

awaken lust within. He that would keep himself free from infection will not come near an infected house. The Nazarite who was forbid wine, might not eat grapes, which might occasion intemperance. Come not near the borders of temptation. Many pray, "Lead us not into temptation", and yet run themselves into temptation.

If you would not be overcome by temptation, be much in prayer. Prayer is the best antidote against temptation. Christ prescribes this remedy, "Watch ye and pray, lest ye enter into temptation" (Mark 14:38). When Paul had a "messenger of Satan to buffet him", he betook himself to prayer. "For this thing I besought the Lord thrice, that it might depart from me" (2 Corinthians 12:8). When Satan assaults furiously let us pray fervently.

If you would not be overcome by temptation, be humble in your own eyes. They are nearest falling who presume on their own strength. The doves, says Pliny, take pride in their flying high, till at last they fly so high, that they become a prey to the hawk; so when men fly high in pride and self-confidence, they become a prey to the tempter.

If you would not be foiled by temptation, do not enter into a dispute with Satan. When Eve began to argue the case with the serpent, the serpent was too hard for her; the devil by his logic disputed her out of Paradise. If you enter into a parley with him, you give him half the victory.

If Adam, in a few hours, sinned himself out of Paradise, how quickly would we sin ourselves into hell, if we were not kept by a greater power than our own! But God puts underneath His everlasting arms. ... Christian, thou canst not believe that evil which is in thy heart, and which will break forth suddenly, if God should leave thee. "Is thy servant a dog that he should do this great thing?" (2 Kings 8:13, 15). Hazael could not believe he had such a root of bitterness in his heart, that he should rip up the women with child. Is thy servant a dog? Yes, and worse than a dog, when that corruption within is stirred up. If one had come to Peter and said, "Peter, within a few hours thou wilt deny Christ", he would have said, "Is thy servant a dog?" But alas! Peter did not know his own heart, nor how far that corruption within would prevail upon him. The sea may be calm and look clear; but when the wind blows, how it rages and foams! so though now thy heart seems good, yet, when temptation blows, how may sin discover itself, making thee foam with lust and passion. Who would have thought to have found adultery in David, and drunkenness in Noah, and cursing in Job? If God leave a man to himself, how suddenly and scandalously may sin break forth in the holiest men on the earth! "I say unto all, Watch" (Mark 13:37). A wandering heart needs a watchful eye.

10.
Contention

"Behold, how good and how pleasant it is for brethren to dwell together in unity! ... for there the LORD commanded the blessing, even life for evermore."—PSALM 133:1, 3

God the Son is called the Prince of Peace (Isaiah 9:6). He came into the world with a song of peace: "On earth peace"; He went out of the world with a legacy of peace, "Peace I leave with you, My peace I give unto you" (John 14:27). Christ's earnest prayer was for peace; He prayed that His people might be one. Christ not only prayed for peace, but bled for peace: "Having made peace through the blood of His cross" (Colossians 1:20). He died not only to make peace between God and man, but between man and man. Christ suffered on the cross, that He might cement Christians together with His blood; as He prayed for peace, so He paid for peace.

If there be but one God, as God is one, so let them that serve Him be one. That is what Christ prayed for. "That they all may be one" (John 17:21). How sad is it to see religion wearing a coat of divers colours; to see Christians of so many opinions, and going so many different ways! It is Satan that has sown these tares of division. He first divided men from God, and then one man from another.

In the primitive times, there was so much love among the godly, as set the heathens a-wondering; and now there is so little, as may set Christians a-blushing.

The saints are Christ's lambs; for a dog to worry a lamb is usual, but for one lamb to worry another is unnatural.

Want of love among Christians doth much silence the Spirit of prayer; hot passions make cold prayers; where animosities and contentions prevail, instead of praying one for another, Christians will be ready to pray one against another.

Why doth the Lord bring His people together in affliction, but to bring them together in affection. Metals will unite in a furnace; if ever Christians unite, it should be in the furnace of affliction. God's rod hath this loud voice in it, "Love one another"; how unworthy is it when Christians are suffering together, to be then striving together!

"Speak not evil one of another" (James 4:11). Unmerciful men know how to boil a quart to a pint; they have the devilish art so to extenuate and lessen the merit of others, that it is even boiled away to nothing. Some, though they have not the power of creation, yet they have the power of annihilation. They can sooner annihilate the good which is in others, than imitate it.

Put on "the breastplate of love" (1 Thessalonians 5:8). This breastplate is insuperable, it may be shot at but it cannot be shot through. "Many waters cannot quench love, neither can the floods drown it."

Love will be the perfume and music of heaven. As perfect love casts out fear, so it casts out envy and discord. Those

CONTENTION

Christians who could not live quietly together on earth (which was the blemish of their profession) in heaven shall be all love; the fire of strife shall cease; there shall be no vilifying, or censuring one another, or raking into one another's sores, but all shall be tied together with the heart-strings of love. Satan cannot put in his cloven foot there to make divisions. There shall be perfect harmony and concord, and not one jarring string in the saint's music.

11. Preaching

"My preaching was not with enticing words of man's wisdom, but in demonstration of the Spirit and of power."

1 Corinthians 2:4

Truth when it is in the plainest dress is most comely. The star shines brightest in its native lustre. Who goes to embroider a pearl? or paint over gold? It is a sign of a wanton Christian to look most at the fringing and garnishing of a truth. Many like the dressing but loathe the food. When men preach rather words than matter, they catch people's ears, not their souls; they do but court, not convert.

To let others go on in sin securely is not charity but cruelty. If a man's house were on fire, and another should see it, and not tell him of it for fear of waking him, were not this cruelty?

Some ministers love to soar aloft, like the eagle, and fly above the people's capacities, endeavouring rather to be admired than understood. Ministers should be stars to give light, not clouds to obscure the truth. It is cruelty to souls when we go about to make easy things hard; this many are guilty of in our age, who go into the pulpit only to tie knots.

If a man were invited to a feast, and there being music at the feast, he should so listen to the music, that he did not mind his meat, you would say, Sure he is not hungry; so when men are for jingling words, and like rather gallantry of speech than spirituality of matter, it is a sign they have surfeited stomachs, and itching ears.

Oftentimes God crowns his labours, and sends most fish into his net, who though he may be less skilful is more faithful; and though he hath less of the brain, yet hath more of the heart.

It is better to have God approve, than the world applaud: there is a time shortly coming when a smile from God's face will be infinitely better than all the applauses of men: how sweet will that word be, "Well done, thou good and faithful servant" (Matthew 25:21).

What pains some men take to go to hell, "They weary themselves to commit iniquity" (Jeremiah 9:5). The devil blows the horn, and men ride post to hell, as if they feared hell would be full ere they should get thither. Do men take all these pains for hell, and shall we not take pains for the kingdom of heaven? The more pains we take for heaven, the more welcome will death be to us. He who has spent his time in serving God, can look death in the face with comfort; he was wholly taken up about heaven, and now he shall be taken up to heaven; he traded before in heaven, and now he shall go to live there.

Christ teaches the heart. Others may teach the ear, Christ the heart. "Whose heart the Lord opened" (Acts 16:14). All that the dispensers of the word can do is but to work knowledge, Christ works grace: they can but give the light of the truth; Christ gives the love of the truth; they can only teach what to believe, Christ teaches how to believe. Christ gives us a taste of the word. Ministers may set the food of the word before you, and carve it out to you; but it is only Christ can cause you to taste it. "If so be ye have tasted that the Lord is gracious" (1 Peter 2:3). "Taste and see that the LORD is good" (Psalm 34:8). It is one thing to hear a truth preached, another thing to taste it. David had got a taste of the word. "Thou hast taught me: how sweet are Thy words to my taste! yea, sweeter than honey to my mouth" (Psalm 119:102-103).

Some speak much of the light of reason improved: alas! the plumb-line of reason is too short to fathom the deep things of God; the light of reason will no more help a man to believe, than the light of a candle will help him to understand.

"The natural man receiveth not the things of the Spirit of God, ... neither can he know them" (1 Corinthians 2:14). He may have more insight into the things of the world than a believer, but he does not see the deep things of God. A swine may see an acorn under a tree, but he cannot see a star.

If you will have the teachings of Christ, walk according to the knowledge you have already. Use your little knowledge well, and Christ will teach you more. "If any man will do His will, he shall know of the doctrine, whether it be of God, or whether I speak of Myself" (John 7:17).

Lay aside those dispositions which may render the preached word ineffectual: As *curiosity*. Some go to hear the word preached, not so much to get grace, as to enrich themselves with notions: having "Itching ears" (2 Timothy 4:3). "Thou art unto them as a very lovely song of one that hath a pleasant voice, and can play well

PREACHING

on an instrument" (Ezekiel 33:32). Many go to the word to feast their ears only; they like the melody of the voice, and the novelty of the opinions (Acts 17:21). This is to love the garnishing of the dish more than the food; it is to desire to be pleased rather than edified. Lay aside *prejudice*. The Sadducees were prejudiced against the doctrine of the resurrection. Sometimes prejudice is against the truths preached, and sometimes against the person preaching. "There is yet one man, Micaiah, ... by whom we may enquire of the LORD, but I hate him" (1 Kings 22:8). This hinders the power of the word. If a patient has an ill opinion of his physician, he will not take any of his medicines, however good they may be. ... Lay aside *covetousness*. Covetousness is not only getting worldly gain unjustly, but loving it inordinately. This is a great hindrance to the preached word. The seed which fell among thorns was choked. The covetous man is thinking on the world when he is hearing; his heart is in his shop. "They sit before thee as My people, and they hear thy words, ... but their heart goeth after their covetousness" (Ezekiel 33:31). Lay aside *partiality*. Partiality in hearing is, when we like to hear some truths preached, but not all. We love to hear of heaven, but not of self-denial; of reigning with Christ, but not of suffering with Him. "Speak unto us smooth things" (Isaiah 30:10), such as may not grate upon the conscience. Many like the comforts of the word, but not its reproofs. Lay aside *censoriousness*. Some, instead of judging themselves for sin, sit as judges upon the preacher; his sermon had either too much gall in it, or it was too long. They would sooner censure a sermon than practise it. Lay aside *disobedience*. "All day long I have stretched forth My hands unto a disobedient and gainsaying people" (Romans 10:21). If, when God speaks to us in His word, we are deaf, when we speak to Him in prayer, He will be dumb.

12. Praying

"Praying always with all prayer and supplication in the Spirit."

EPHESIANS 6:18

A godly man is a praying man. "Every one that is godly shall pray unto Thee." As soon as grace is poured in, prayer is poured out. Prayer is the soul's traffic with heaven; God comes down to us by His Spirit, and we go up to Him by prayer.

A spiritual prayer is a believing prayer: "Whatsoever ye shall ask in prayer, believing, ye shall receive" (Matthew 21:22). The reason why so many prayers suffer shipwreck, is because they split against the rock of unbelief; praying without faith is shooting without bullets.

A spiritual prayer is an holy prayer: Wherefore lift up holy hands (1 Timothy 2:8). Prayer must be offered on the altar of a pure heart; sin lived in makes the heart hard, and God's ear deaf; sin stops the mouth of prayer, it doth as the thief to the traveller, puts a gag in his mouth, that he cannot speak; "If I regard iniquity in my heart, the Lord will not hear me" (Psalm 66:18). It is foolish to pray against sin, and then to sin against prayer.

A spiritual prayer is an humble prayer: "LORD, thou hast heard the desire of the humble" (Psalm 10:17). Prayer is the asking of an alms, which requires humility. It is comely to see a poor nothing lie at the feet of its Maker; "Behold, I have taken upon me to speak unto the Lord, which am but dust and ashes" (Genesis 18:27). The lower the heart descends, the higher the prayer ascends. God accepts broken expressions, when they come from broken hearts.

A spiritual prayer is when we have spiritual ends in prayer. There is a vast difference between a spiritual prayer, and a carnal desire: the ends of a hypocrite are carnal; he looks a-squint in prayer; it is not the sense of his spiritual wants that moves him, but rather lust; "Ye ask amiss, that ye may consume it upon your lusts" (James 4:3). The sinner prays more for food than grace; this God doth not interpret praying, but howling. "They howled upon their beds: they assemble themselves for corn and wine" (Hosea 7:14). Prayers which want a good aim want a good answer. A godly man drives the trade of prayer that he may increase the stock of grace.

Prayer delights God's ear, it melts His heart, it opens His hand: God cannot deny a praying soul.

How hard is it sometimes to get leave of hearts to seek God! Jesus Christ went more willingly to the cross than we do to the throne of grace.

Christ was in an agony at prayer (Luke 22:44). Many when they pray are rather in a lethargy, than in an agony. When they are about the world, they are all fire; when they are at prayer, they are all ice.

The joint stock of the prayers of saints works for good to the godly. "Prayer was made without ceasing of the church unto God for him. … And, behold, the angel of the Lord came upon him … and raised him up, … and his chains fell off" (Acts 12:5-7). The angel fetched Peter out of prison, but it was prayer fetched the angel.

"Effectual fervent prayer prevails much" (James 5:16). Cold prayers, like cold suitors, never speed. Prayer without fervency, is like a sacrifice without a fire. Prayer is called a "pouring out of the soul", to signify vehemence (1 Samuel 1:15). Formality starves prayer.

If you would keep your mind fixed in prayer, keep your eye fixed. "Unto Thee lift I up mine eyes, O Thou that dwellest in the heavens" (Psalm 123:1). Much vanity comes in at the eye. When the eye wanders in prayer, the heart wanders. Love is a great fixer of the thoughts. He who is in love cannot keep his thoughts off the object. He who loves the world has his thoughts upon the world. Did we love God more, our minds would be more intent upon Him in prayer. He who gives himself liberty to have vain thoughts out of prayer, will scarcely have other thoughts in prayer.

He that leaves off prayer leaves off to fear God. "Thou castest off fear, and restrainest prayer before God" (Job 15:4). A man that has left off prayer is fit for any wickedness. When Saul had given over inquiring after God he went to the witch of Endor.

Faith is the breath of prayer; prayer is dead unless faith breathe in it. "Let him ask in faith" (James 1:6). "Whatsoever ye shall ask in prayer, believing, ye shall receive" (Matthew 21:22). Without faith it is speaking, not praying. Faith must take prayer by the hand, or there is no coming nigh to God. A faithless prayer is fruitless. "They could not enter in because of unbelief", is as true of prayer; it cannot enter into heaven because of unbelief.

13.
Meditation

"His delight is in the law of the LORD; and in His law doth he meditate day and night."—PSALM 1:2

Meditation is the soul's retiring of itself, that by a serious and solemn thinking upon God, the heart may be raised up to heavenly affections.

MEDITATION OPPOSED BY THE DEVIL

The devil is an enemy to meditation; he cares not how much people read and hear, nor how little they meditate; he knows that meditation is a means to compose the heart, and to bring it into a gracious frame; now the devil is against that; Satan is content that you should be hearing and praying Christians, so that ye be not meditating Christians; he can stand your small shot, provided that you do not put in this bullet.

MEDITATION HINDERED BY THE WORLD

A Christian when he goes to meditate, must lock up himself from the world. The world spoils meditation; Christ went "apart" into the mount to pray, so go apart when you are to meditate; "Isaac went out to meditate in the field" (Genesis 24:63). He sequestered and retired himself that he might take a walk with God by meditation. The world's music will either play us asleep, or distract us in our meditations. When a mote is gotten into the eye, it hinders the sight; when worldly thoughts, as motes, are gotten into the mind, which is the eye of the soul, it cannot look up so stedfastly to heaven by contemplation. When Abraham went to sacrifice he left his servant and the ass at the bottom of the hill (Genesis 22:5), so, when a Christian is going up the hill of meditation, he should leave all secular cares at the bottom of the hill, that he may be alone, and take a turn in heaven. This is the first thing, lock and bolt the door against the world.

MEDITATION HINDERED BY ROVING THOUGHTS

There must be in meditation a fixing the heart upon the object; carnal Christians are like quicksilver which cannot be made to fix; their thoughts are roving up and down and will not fix; like the bird that hops from one bough to another, and stays nowhere. David was a man fit to meditate: "O God, my heart is fixed" (Psalm 108:1). In meditation there must be a staying of the thoughts upon the object: "Mary kept all these things, and pondered them in her heart" (Luke 2:19).

MEDITATION AND MEMORY

The meditation of a thing hath more sweetness in it than the bare remembrance. The memory is the chest or cupboard to lock up a truth, meditation is the palate to feed on it. When David began to meditate on God, it was sweet to him as marrow (Psalm 63:5-6). There is as much difference between a truth remembered, and a truth meditated on, as between a cordial in a glass, and a cordial drunk down.

MEDITATION

MEDITATION AND STUDY

Meditation and study differ. Study is a work of the brain, meditation of the heart; study sets the invention on work, meditation sets the affection on work. Study is the finding out of a truth, meditation is the spiritual improvement of a truth; the one searcheth for the vein of gold, the other digs out the gold. Study is like a winter sun that hath little warmth and influence: meditation leaves one in a holy frame: it melts the heart when it is frozen, and makes it drop into tears of love.

THE NECESSITY OF MEDITATION

Without meditation the truth of God will not stay with us; the heart is hard, and the memory slippery, and without meditation all is lost; meditation imprints and fastens a truth in the mind. Without meditation the truths which we know will never affect our hearts, "These words which I command thee this day shall be in thine heart" (Deuteronomy 6:6). How can the word be in the heart, unless it be wrought in by meditation? As an hammer drives a nail to the head, so meditation drives a truth to the heart. Without meditation the word preached may increase notion, not affection. Meditation fetcheth life in a truth. There are many truths lie, as it were, in the heart dead, which when we meditate upon, they begin to have light and heat in them.

THE TIME FOR MEDITATION

The best time to converse with God is, before worldly occasions stand knocking at the door to be let in: the morning is, as it were, the cream of the day, let the cream be taken off, and let God have it. Wind up thy heart towards heaven in the beginning of the day, and it will go the better all the day after. He that loseth his heart in the morning in the world, will hardly find it again all the day.

O! Christians, let God have your morning meditations. He takes it in disdain to have the world served before Him. Suppose a king and a yeoman were to dine in the same room, and to sit at two tables; if the yeoman should have his meat brought up, and be served first, the king might take it in high disdain, and look upon it as a contempt done to his person. When the world shall be served first, all our morning thoughts attending it, and the Lord shall be put off with the dregs of the day, is not this a contempt done to the God of glory? God deserves the first of our thoughts; some of His first thoughts were upon us; we had a being in His thoughts before we had a being; He thought upon us "before the foundations of the world." Before we fell He was thinking how to raise us. We had the morning of His thoughts. We have taken up His thoughts from eternity: if we have had some of God's first thoughts, well may He have our first thoughts. "In the morning the dew fell" (Exodus 16:13). The dew of a blessing falls early; now we are likeliest to have God's company. If you would meet with a friend, you go betimes in the morning before he be gone out. I would not by this, wholly exclude evening meditation. Isaac went out to meditate in the eventide (Genesis 24:63). When business is over, and everything calm, it is good to take a turn with God in the evening. God had his evening sacrifice, as well as His morning (Exodus 29:39), as the cream at the top is sweet, so the sugar at the bottom.

The length of time to meditate

Meditate till thou findest thy heart grow warm. If when a man is cold, you ask how long he should stand by the fire? Sure, till he be thoroughly warm, and made fit for his work. So, Christian, thy heart is cold; never a day, no, not the hottest day in summer, but it freezeth there; now stand at the fire of meditation till thou findest thy affections warmed, and thou art made fit for spiritual service. David mused till his heart waxed hot within him: "While I was musing the fire burned" (Psalm 39:3).

THE GAIN OF MEDITATION

Meditation is an excellent means to profit by the word: reading may bring a truth into the head, meditation brings it into the heart; better meditate on one sermon than hear five. There is a disease in children called the rickets, when they have great heads, but their lower parts are small and thrive not. I wish many professors have not the spiritual rickets, they have great heads, much knowledge, but yet they thrive not in godliness, their heart is faint, their feet feeble, they walk not vigorously in the ways of God; and the cause of this disease is, the want of meditation. Illumination without meditation makes us no better than devils. Satan is an angel of light, yet black enough.

Meditation doth make the heart serious. Some Christians have light hearts: "Her prophets are light" (Zephaniah 3:4). A light Christian will be blown into any opinion or vice; you may blow a feather any way: there are many feathery Christians; the devil no sooner comes with a temptation but they are ready to take fire; now meditation makes the heart serious. Meditation consolidates a Christian; solid gold is best; the solid Christian is the only metal that will pass current with God.

Meditation is the bellows of the affections. We light affection at this fire of meditation, "while I was musing the fire burned" (Psalm 39:3). Illumination makes us shining lamps, meditation makes us burning lamps.

Meditation fits for prayer. Meditation first furnisheth with matter to pray, and then furnisheth with a heart to pray. "I muse on the work of Thy hands, I stretch forth my hands unto Thee" (Psalm 143:5-6). The musing of his head made way for the stretching forth of his hands in prayer. Prayer is the child of meditation: meditation leads the van, and prayer brings up the rear.

Meditation is a strong antidote against sin; sin puts a worm into conscience, a sting into death, a fire into hell; did men meditate of this, that after all their dainty dishes, death will bring in the reckoning in hell, they would say as David in another sense, ""Let me not eat of their dainties" (Psalm 141:4). The devil's apple hath a bitter core.

Meditation is an excellent means to lessen our esteem of the world. Great things seem little to him that stands high, if he could live among the stars, the earth would seem as nothing. He who is catching at a crown, will not fish for gudgeons, as Cleopatra once said to Mark Antony.

DIRECTIONS FOR MEDITATION

Read before you meditate. "Give attendance to reading" (1 Timothy 4:13). Then it follows, "meditate on these things" (verse 15). Reading doth furnish with matter; it is the oil that feeds the lamp of meditation. Be sure your meditations are founded upon Scripture. Reading without meditation is unfruitful; meditation without reading is dangerous.

Meditate not on too many things at once. One truth driven home by meditation will most kindly affect the heart. Drive but one wedge of meditation at a time, but be sure you drive it home to the heart. Those who aim at a whole flock of birds hit none.

Pray over your meditations. Prayer fastens meditation upon the soul; prayer is a-tying a knot at the end of meditation that it doth not slip.

MEDITATION

Let meditation be reduced to practice. Live over your meditation. "This book of the law shall not depart out of thy mouth; but thou shalt meditate therein day and night, that thou mayest observe *to do* according to all the law" (Joshua 1:8). Meditation and practice, like two sisters, must go hand in hand. The end of meditation is action. They who meditate in God's law, and observe not to do, are no better than the devil; he knows much, but still he is a devil.

14. Departing

"The time of my departure is at hand."—2 Timothy 4:6

"To depart, and to be with Christ; which is far better."

Philippians 1:23

"But this I say, brethren, the time is short" (1 Corinthians 7:29). If we reckon that for time which is well spent, then time is brought into a narrow compass indeed: a great part of our time lies fallow: take from our life all the time of eating, drinking, sleeping, besides idle impertinencies, and then how short is our time! How little is the time wherein we can truly say, *Hoc vixi*, This time I have lived! O how little is the time *lived*, but time *lost*. The time is short, why should we love that over-much which we cannot keep over-long?

The world rings changes, it is never constant but in its disappointments. The world is but a great inn, where we are to stay a night or two, and be gone; what madness is it so to set our heart upon our inn, as to forget our home?

The world is a great inn; we are guests in this inn. Travellers when they are met in their inn, do not spend all their time in speaking about their inn; they are to lodge

DEPARTING

there but a few hours, and they are gone; but they are speaking of their home, and the country whither they are travelling. So when we meet together, we should not be talking only about the world; we are to leave this presently; but we should talk of our heavenly country (Hebrews 11:16).

We are travellers who take up our lodgings here for a night; and Paul longed to be out of his inn. "I am in a strait betwixt two, having a desire to depart, and to be with Christ; which is far better" (Philippians 1:23). The apostle doth not say, "I must depart"; but, "I desire to depart." All men must depart. There is a dying principle in all. Nebuchadnezzar's image, though it had a head of gold, yet had feet of clay (Daniel 2:43). The strongest man stands upon feet of clay, and must moulder away in time; death will come at last.

The apostle doth not say, Having a desire to die, but "to depart". What a wicked man fears, a godly man hopes for. "I desire", saith Paul, "to depart"; a sinner cries, "I am loath to depart." David calls death a going out of the world (Psalm 39:13). A wicked man doth not go out, but is dragged out. If a wicked man were put to his choice, he would never come where God is; but would choose the serpent's curse, to eat dust (Genesis 3:14), but not to return to dust. A soul enlivened with grace, looks upon the world as a wilderness, wherein are fiery serpents, and he desires to get out of this wilderness. Simeon, having taken Christ in his arms, cries out, "Lord, now lettest thou Thy servant depart in peace" (Luke 2:29). He that hath taken Christ into the arms of his faith, will sing Simeon's song, "Lord, let Thy servant depart." The bird desires to go out of the cage, though it be made of gold.

Death will dry up a believer's tears: "And God shall wipe away all tears from their eyes" (Revelation 7:17). Weeping is nothing but a cloud of sorrow gathered in the heart, dropping into water. Ever since we looked upon the tree of knowledge, our eyes have watered. Death shall stop the bottle of tears, and open the gate of paradise. A believer's dying day is his ascension day to glory.

The apostle had three great desires, and they were all centred in Christ. One was to be found in Christ (Philippians 3:9); the other was to magnify Christ (Philippians 1:20); the third was to be with Christ (Philippians 1:23). Paul doth not say, I desire to depart, and be in heaven, but to be with Christ. It is Christ's presence makes heaven. It is not the cherubim or seraphim which make paradise; but "the Lamb is the light thereof" (Revelation 21:23).

There had been little comfort in departing, if the apostle had not put in this word, "to be with Christ". Death will make a glorious change to a believer; it is but crossing the Dead Sea, and he shall be with Christ. Death to a child of God is like the whirlwind to the prophet Elijah; it blew off his mantle, but carried the prophet up to heaven: so death is a boisterous wind which blows off the mantle of the flesh (for the body is but the mantle the soul is wrapped in), but it carries the soul up to Christ; the day of a believer's dissolution is the day of his coronation. Though death be a bitter cup, there is sugar at the bottom. Though the flesh calls death the last enemy (1 Corinthians 15:26), yet faith calls it the best friend; it brings a man to Christ, which is far better.

To be with Christ implies we shall see Him as He is; here we see Him but through a glass darkly. To be with Christ implies we shall not only see Him but enjoy Him: "Enter thou into the joy of thy Lord" (Matthew 25:21); not only

DEPARTING

see it, but enter into it. To be with Christ implies duration; "So shall we ever be with the Lord" (1 Thessalonians 4:17). "The fashion of this world passeth away" (1 Corinthians 7:31). Earthly comforts, though they may be sweet, they are swift; but this privilege of being with Christ, runs parallel with eternity: "So shall we ever be with the Lord."

To a believer it is a happy departing; to a wicked man it is a sad departing, there is nothing but departing; he departs out of this life, and he departs from Christ: "Depart from Me, ye cursed" (Matthew 25:41).

If we are in Christ while we live, we shall go to Christ while we die. We must be in Christ before we can be with Christ.

This is that which makes heaven to be heaven, "We shall be ever with the Lord."

"Enter thou into the joy of thy Lord" (Matthew 25:21). O amazing! The saints enter into God's own joy: they have not only the joy which God bestows, but the joy which God enjoys.

He is a constant Friend. "His compassions fail not" (Lamentations 3:22). God is a friend for ever. "Having loved His own, He loved them unto the end" (John 13:1). He loves to the end, and there is no end of that love. How invincible is the love of Christ! "It is strong as death" (Canticles [Song of Songs] 8:6). Death might take away His life, not this love. And that which makes this love of Christ the more stupendous, there was nothing in us to excite or draw forth His love: He did not love us because we were worthy, but by loving us He made us worthy.

Christ's love did not cease at the hour of death. We write on our letters, "Your friend till death"; but Christ wrote in another style, "Your friend after death." Christ died once, but lives ever. He is now testifying His affection for us, He is interceding for us. When He hath done dying, yet He hath not done loving.

"Enter thou into the joy of thy Lord" (Matthew 25:21). Here joy enters into the saints; in heaven they enter into joy. There can be no more sorrow in heaven than there is joy in hell.

Why should we shed tears immoderately for them who have tears wiped from their eyes? Why should we be swallowed up of grief for them who are swallowed up of joy? They are gone to their kingdom; they are not lost but gone a little before; not perished, but translated.

Death may take away a few worldly comforts, but it gives that which is better; it takes away a short lease and gives land of inheritance. If the saints possess a kingdom when they die, they have no cause to fear death. A prince would not be afraid to cross the sea, though tempestuous, if he were sure to be crowned as soon as he came to shore.

15.
Crowning

"I have fought a good fight, I have finished my course, I have kept the faith: henceforth there is laid up for me a crown of righteousness, which the Lord, the righteous Judge, shall give me at that day."— 2 TIMOTHY 4:7-8

We must run the race before we wear the crown. If you set the crown on Christ's head while you live, He will set the crown on your head when you die.

Behold, what manner of love is this, that Christ should be *arraigned* and we *adorned*, that the curse should be laid on His head and the crown set on ours.

"Henceforth there is laid up for me a crown of righteousness." A Christian's best things are to come. We are here as Princes in disguise, the world knoweth us not; but there is a crown laid up. While we are *laying out* for God, He is *laying up* for us.

If you would wear the crown of righteousness, then walk in the way of righteousness. "In the way of righteousness is life" (Proverbs 12:28). But, alas, this is a very untrodden way.

Some *know* the way of righteousness but do not walk in it.

Others *commend* the way of righteousness, but do not walk in it.

Others instead of walking in the way, they are good only at *crossing* the way; they oppose the way of righteousness; such are persecutors.

Others walk a few steps in the way and then go back again. These are apostates, as if they were going to heaven backwards.

Others walk half in the way and half out: these are loose professors who under a notion of Christian liberty do walk carelessly, crying up justification that they may weaken the power of sanctification. Surely were there none other Bible to read in, but the lives of some professors, we should read but little Scripture there.

Others instead of walking in the way do traduce and slander the way of righteousness. The way of truth shall be evil spoken of (2 Peter 2:2).

Others *creep* in the way, they do not walk; they go on but very slow. Those who look on can hardly tell whether they make any progress or no.

O! all you that would wear the crown of righteousness, walk in the way of righteousness; walk so that if we could suppose the Bible to be lost, it might be found again in your lives.

If you would wear the crown of righteousness, put on the armour of righteousness (2 Corinthians 6:7). If you will have this crown you must fight for it (2 Timothy 4:7-8).

"The time is short", saith the apostle. We are ready to strike sail, we are almost ashore, and then we shall be crowned. The crown is hard by, you sail apace ... Though we bear the *cross*, we shall wear the *crown*.

A Christian's work is soon over, but not his reward. How great is that reward which thoughts cannot measure, nor time finish.

In the future life the saints shall be out of the noise of the drum and cannon, and not one stroke shall be struck more; then shall they not appear in their *armour*, but their *white robes*.

The cross is heavy, but the sharper the cross, the brighter the crown.

"Love never faileth" (1 Corinthians 13:8). Faith is the staff we walk with in this life. "We walk by faith" (2 Corinthians 5:7). But we shall set this staff at heaven's door, and only love shall enter.

Heaven itself is not a saint's reward. "Whom have I in heaven but Thee?" (Psalm 73:25).

"Hold up my goings in Thy paths that my footsteps slip not" (Psalm 17:5). "Lord, hold me up that I may hold out. Thou hast set the crown at the end of the race, let me run the race, that I may wear the crown"; it was Beza's prayer, and let it be ours, "Lord, perfect what Thou hast begun in me, that I may not suffer shipwreck when I am almost at the haven."

Love takes possession of glory, but faith gives a title to it. Love is the crowning grace in heaven, but faith is the conquering grace upon earth. "This is the victory that overcometh the world, even our faith."

"Now is our salvation nearer than when we believed" (Romans 13:11). You are within a few days' march of heaven. Salvation is near to you. Christians, it is but a while and you will have done weeping and praying, and be triumphing; you shall put off your mourning, and put on white robes; you shall put off your armour, and put on a victorious crown.

Heaven's glory only is commensurate to the vast desires of an immortal soul. The soul is never satisfied till it has God for its portion, and heaven for its haven. The glory of heaven is pure and unmixed. There gold has no alloy. There the rose of Sharon grows without thorns. There is ease without pain, honour without disgrace, life without death. Physicians there are out of date: no distemper there, no passing bell, or bill of mortality. "Neither can they die any more" (Luke 20:36).

The glory is distributed to every saint. In an earthly kingdom the crown goes but to one, a crown will fit but one head; but above the crown goes to all (Revelation 1:6). All the elect are kings. The land is settled chiefly upon the heir, but in heaven all the saints are heirs. "Heirs of God, and co-heirs with Christ" (Romans 8:17). God has land enough to give to all His heirs.

16.
Fragments

"A word fitly spoken is like apples of gold in pictures of silver."

PROVERBS 25:11

Only the believer is the rich man; here is his estate summed up, "All things are his."

The creation is but a theatre to act the great work of redemption upon.

Christ was not only "a Lamb without spot" but "a Lamb slain". Every pardon a sinner hath, is written in Christ's blood.

If we will needs be high-minded, let it be in setting our mind upon heavenly things.

If thou wouldest get Christ into thy heart, let heaven be in thine eye: "Set your affections upon things above" (Colossians 3:2). There needs no exhortation to set our hearts on things below.

Though grace cannot be lost, yet it may be hid. David so clouded his graces by sin, that others could hardly see the cloth of gold under the filthy garments.

Why is prayer so sweet, but because the soul hath private conference with Christ? Why is the word precious but because it is a means to convey Christ? An ordinance without Christ, is but feeding upon the dish instead of the meat.

Here Christ puts His graces upon His spouse, in heaven He will put His glory upon her.

Such was Adam's ambition to know more, that by tasting the tree of knowledge, he lost the tree of life.

Unity in Trinity, and Trinity in Unity, where one makes three, and three make but one: this is bad arithmetic, but good divinity.

Divisions are Satan's powder-plot to blow up religion.

The godly man hath all his best things to come; the wicked man hath all his worst things to come: as their way is different so their end.

Do not so look upon your troubles as to forget your mercies.

He that is proud of his knowledge, the devil cares not how much he knows.

How many have pulled down their souls to build up their houses.

God can strike a straight stroke by a crooked stick.

Let who will rule, God over-rules.

God can with a word unpin the wheels, and break the axle-tree of the creation. He can stop the lion's mouth, cause the sun to stand still, and make the fire not burn.

How slow is God to anger. He was longer in destroying Jericho, than in making the world.

Christ will not throw away His pearls for every speck of dirt.

Christ shed tears for them that shed His blood.

Our nature is defiled; how then can the actions be pure? If the water be foul in the well, it cannot be clean in the bucket. "We are all as an unclean thing" (Isaiah 64:6).

That which begins in hypocrisy ends in apostacy.

Eternity to the godly is a day which hath no sun-setting; and to the wicked, a night which hath no sun-rising.

Now is the time of God's long-suffering, after death will be the time of the sinner's long suffering.

Take heed lest by growing rich, you grow worth nothing at last.

Many live to see their names buried before them.

"When I awake I am still with Thee" (Psalm 139:18). If you would still be with God, watch over your hearts every day; lock up your hearts with God every morning, and give Him the key.

Toleration is the grave of reformation. By toleration we adopt other men's sins, and make them our own.

God loves a broken heart, not a divided heart.

If a wicked man seems to have peace at death, it is not from the knowledge of his happiness, but from the ignorance of his danger.

It will be so much the worse to go to hell with hopes of heaven.

An idle person is a fit subject for the devil to work upon.

God must light up the lamp of grace in the heart; weeds grow of themselves, flowers are planted.

Godliness is glory in the seed, and glory is godliness in the flower.

Look upon an humble Saviour, and let the plumes of pride fall.

A godly man is an heavenly man; heaven is in him, before he is in heaven.

Other friends thou canst not keep, God is a friend thou canst not lose; He will be thy guide in life, thy hope in death, thy reward after death.

Many parents are careful to lay up portions for their children, but they do not lay up prayers for them.

We are apt to forget three things — our faults, our friends, our instructions.

True faith will trust God where it cannot trace Him.

Such sheep as have most wool are soonest fleeced.

It is good to find out our sins, lest they find us out.

Our life is a wayfaring life and a warfaring life.

Affliction is a bitter root, but it bears sweet fruit.

"Surely the wrath of man shall praise Thee" (Psalm 76:10). He can reap His glory out of men's fury.

True love is not only at the tongue's end, but at the finger's end; it is the labour of love.

Does Christ appear for us in heaven, and are we afraid to appear for Him on earth?

It is Satan that makes us have good thoughts of ourselves, and hard thoughts of God.

As we must answer to God for idle words, so for sinful silence.

FRAGMENTS

As the glass shows what the face is, whether it be fair or foul, so the words show what the heart is.

Did our thoughts dwell above we should live sweeter lives. The higher the lark flies the sweeter the songs.

Heaven is a place where sorrow cannot live and joy cannot die.

'Tis vain to speak of hopes of salvation and yet have the marks of damnation.

The world is a flattering enemy, it kills with embracing ... whom the world kisseth it betrayeth.

The way to overcome is upon our knees.

The world is enough to busy us, not to fill us. "In the fulness of his sufficiency he shall be in straits" (Job 20:22).

Immorality begins at infidelity (Hebrews 3:12).

Do you love to see Christ's picture in a saint, though hung in never so poor a frame?

Be more afraid of sin than of suffering.

Is heaven in thine eye, and Christ in thy heart, and the world under thy feet?

How many have perished by being their own saviours.

To render evil for evil is brutish; to render evil for good is devilish; to render good for evil is Christian.

None so empty of grace as he that thinks he is full.

Such as would be over-rich, will over-reach.

It is a poor thing to have an applauding world and an accusing conscience.

Saints have their infirmities; but the wicked do not hate them for these, but for their holiness.

Whatever you deny for Christ, you shall find again in Christ.

The sins you commit in haste you will repent at leisure.

Prayer keeps the heart open to God and shut to sin.

"Gideon took thorns of the wilderness, and briers, and with them he taught the men of Succoth" (Judges 8:16). God by the thorns and briers of affliction teaches us.

God gives gracious supports in affliction. If He strikes with one hand, He supports with the other. "Underneath are the everlasting arms" (Deuteronomy 33:27).

Prosperity exposes to much evil: it is hard to carry a full cup without spilling, and a full estate without sinning.

God lets us fall into sufferings to prevent falling into snares.

Why should we think to tread only upon roses and violets, when prophets and apostles have marched through briers to heaven?

If a man begins his voyage to heaven in the storm of death, it is a thousand to one if he does not suffer eternal shipwreck.

Pride stops the current of gratitude. A proud man will never be thankful; he looks upon all he has either to be of his own procuring or deserving.

Many pray Agur's first prayer, "Give me not poverty", but few pray his last prayer, "Give me not riches" (Proverbs 30:8).

They that sleep in seedtime, will beg in harvest.

The prayer which wants a good aim wants a good issue.

FRAGMENTS

God's rod is a pencil to draw Christ's image more distinctly upon us.

Affliction is God's flail to thresh off the husks, not to consume the precious grain.

Fiery trials make golden Christians (Proverbs 17:3).

God only threshes the precious wheat, but He burns the useless chaff. He chastens the righteous, but He condemns the wicked.

The jewel of assurance is best kept in the cabinet of an humble heart.

Christ is never sweet until sin is felt to be bitter.

At Christ's death "the rocks rent". Not to be affected with Christ's dying love, is to have hearts harder than rocks.

Conscience is like a bee; use it well, and it will give honey; use it ill, and it will put forth a sting.

A troubled conscience is the first-fruit of hell.

Eternity is a sea without bottom or banks, for what line or plummet can fathom its depths?

A heathen, exercising much cruelty to a Christian, asked him, in scorn, what great miracle his Master, Jesus Christ, ever did. The Christian replied, "This miracle, that although you use me thus, I can forgive you."

Grace is Christ's portrait drawn on the soul.

He that sins because of God's mercy, shall have judgment without mercy.

Where grace grows sin cannot thrive.

God makes grace flourish most in the fall of the leaf. "They shall still bring forth in old age" (Psalm 92:14).

The sinner may live in a calm, but he will die in a storm. He that lives graceless, dies peaceless.

He who has no faith in his heart will have no fear of God before his eyes.

He who believes not in the blood of the Lamb, must feel the wrath of the Lamb.

Sin unrepented of ends in a tragedy. It has the devil for its father, shame for its companion, and death for its wages.

When people do not mind what God speaks to them in His word, God as little minds what they say to Him in prayer.

The godly have some good in them, therefore the devil afflicts them; and some evil in them, therefore God afflicts them.

A sinner's heart is the devil's mansion-house. "I will return unto my house" (Matthew 12:44).

A sinner grinds in the devil's mill. "The lusts of your father ye will do" (John 8:44).

EXTRACTS FROM THE WRITINGS OF THOMAS WATSON

www.ingramcontent.com/pod-product-compliance
Lightning Source LLC
Chambersburg PA
CBHW032148040426
42449CB00005B/446